50 DAYS

TO TRANSFORMATION

TRAIN TO REIGN AS CHRIST'S ETERNAL HEIR

BARBARA ANN JETER
MANDY ARLEDGE
NISE DAVIES

Cover Design & Page Design: Bayley Holt @ bayleyholtdesigns.com

Editing: Ashley Hagan @ Inkwellwriters.com

ISBN: 9798985693409

ISBN: 9798985693416

EternalHeiress.org

Scripture quotations are taken from the King James Version of the Bible unless otherwise noted.

The Holy Bible, King James Version. Cambridge Edition: 1769; King James Bible Online, 2022. www.kingjamesbibleonline.org.

In Loving Memory of Courtney Cordes

TABLE OF CONTENTS

Introduction..x

Salvation is for You...xi

Week 1: I am Brilliant

Mountains...3

Day 01..5

Day 02..9

Day 03..13

Day 04..17

Day 05..21

Day 06..25

Day 07..29

Week 2: I am Bold

Day 08..35

Day 09..39

Day 10..43

Day 11..47

Day 12..51

Day 13..55

Day 14..59

Week 3: I am Brave

Day 15..65

Day 16..69

Day 17..73

Day 18..77

Day 19..81

Day 20..85

Day 21..89

Week 4: I am Beloved

Day 22..95

Day 23..99

Day 24..103

Day 25..107

Day 26..111

Day 27..115

Day 28..119

Week 5: I am Blessed

Day 29..125

Day 30..129

Day 31..133

Day 32..137

Day 33..141

Day 34..145

Day 35..149

Week 6: I am a Son of a Good Father

Day 36..155

Day 37..159

Day 38..163

Day 39..167

Day 40..171

Day 41..175

Day 42..179

Week 7: I am an Heir of a Great King

Day 43..185

Day 44..189

Day 45..193

Day 46..197

Day 47..201

Day 48..205

Day 49..209

Day 50..213

About The Authors..217

Acknowledgments...219

INTRODUCTION

Welcome to seven weeks of transformation! This journey is intended to help you see how loved and special you are to God. Understanding more of your potential in Christ helps you continue choosing transformation.

Each day, repeat out loud the Eternal Heir Affirmation found before every new chapter. These are true statements to help you fully embrace all that God has created you to be!

**IN CHRIST,
I AM BRILLIANT
I AM BOLD
I AM BRAVE
I AM BLESSED
I AM BELOVED
I AM
A SON OF A GOOD FATHER
AND AN
HEIR OF A GREAT KING**

To "transform" means to change in form, appearance, structure, condition, nature, or character. Complete transformation includes changing spirit, soul, and body.

This transformation begins with salvation. If you're not sure about your salvation, read "Salvation is for YOU" on the following page. Also read it if you would like to refocus and rededicate your life to God.

As you travel this transforming journey, each day has a scripture and devotional followed by: The Challenge, Meditation/Journal, The Prayer, and The Transformation.

Learn and put what you learn into practice. Daily.

SALVATION IS FOR YOU

Who? Me?

Yes, YOU!!

You see, THE God of the universe created you. Before the foundations of the world, He knew you. He loved you. He created you for a purpose—to love and be loved by Him.

"Just as He chose us in Him before the foundation of the world, that we should be holy and without blame before Him in love" (Ephesians 1:4 NKJV).

After He created the perfect world, the enemy snuck in with lies to trick us humans into betraying our creator, God.

Adam was the first human God created. He and his wife, Eve, were created perfectly. They got to live in a perfect garden and have walk-n-talks with God every day…until they listened to Satan. Once that happened, mankind has never been the same.

Satan, the father of lies, told us to disobey God. He wanted us to become our own gods, to know good and evil for ourselves, and not depend on God to tell us anything.

Once humans, through Adam, chose to betray God, we were open to shame, guilt, pride, fear, and every other lie. Ouch! Those lies have been destroying lives ever since.

You see, Adam chose for us. Even though God said death would be the consequence, Adam still made the decision to disobey. It's been a broken world ever since.

Because God is pure and perfect, He had to put a barrier between our sinful natures and His holiness. God is just. A price needed to be paid for the sin.

BUT…

God is LOVE. In fact, He loved us so much, that He sent His perfect Son, Jesus Christ, to die for our sins.

"For God so loved the world, that he gave his only begotten Son, that whosoever believeth in him should not perish, but have everlasting life" (John 3:16).

Two thousand years ago, Jesus Christ, the Son of God, came to Earth as a human baby, born to Mary, a virgin. His humble birth in a stable in Bethlehem was the answer to God's promise to save us.

Sadly, He had to die on a cross to pay for our sins. After just thirty-three years on Earth, He laid down His life. Only a perfect, pure sacrifice could replace our deserved sentence of eternal death and separation from LOVE.

"For if, when we were enemies, we were reconciled to God by the death of his Son, much more, being reconciled, we shall be saved by his life…Wherefore, as by one man sin entered into the world, and death by sin; and so death passed upon all men, for that all have sinned…" (Romans 5:10, 12).

Because of God's perfect plan driven by His overwhelming love, we can live with hope for complete redemption through the blood of Jesus…a God-sized payment for the sins of all humanity. We only have to believe.

"And they said, Believe on the Lord Jesus Christ, and thou shalt be saved, and thy house" (Acts 16:31).

By the way, I'm not talking about "religion." The enemy has distorted the truth of salvation through many religions. I'm talking about a relationship with LOVE.

"Beloved, let us love one another: for love is of God; and every one that loveth is born of God, and knoweth God. He that loveth not knoweth not God; for God is love. In this was manifested the love of God toward us, because that God sent his only begotten Son into the world, that we might live through him" (1 John 4:7-9).

You might say, "But you don't know what I've done. Or how bad I've been. Or how unworthy I feel. Or how messed up I am. Or what I've been told. Or who's hurt me. I don't deserve salvation. God would never want me."

"For all have sinned, and come short of the glory of God; being justified freely by his grace through the redemption that is in Christ Jesus" (Romans 3:23-24).

Everyone has sinned; you are not alone! But grace means we get a pardon we didn't earn—a spiritual get-out-of-jail card that we don't deserve. Oh, but God…He freely gives us salvation because Jesus already paid the price.

Eternal life is available when we surrender our sins and our mess to God. It's as simple as owning our sins, repenting, and asking Jesus to be Lord in our lives. Wow!

"If we confess our sins, he is faithful and just to forgive us our sins and to cleanse us from all unrighteousness" (1 John 1:9).

In an instant, those sins are all gone and no longer held against us—paid for in full and forgiven by the blood of God's Son, Jesus.

"As far as the east is from the west, so far hath he removed our transgressions (sins) from us" (Psalm 103:12).

What happens next? We get to start learning about the God we just chose to have a relationship with…a relationship based on honesty, grace, forgiveness, and love.

"For I am persuaded, that neither death, nor life, nor angels, nor principalities, nor powers, nor things present, nor things to come, nor height, nor depth, nor any other creature, shall be able to separate us from the love of God, which is in Christ Jesus our Lord" (Romans 8:38, 39).

If you're not sure you believe any of this, just ask God to make Himself real to you. If He is actually the all-powerful God, He can make Himself real to you. Really! How will you know it's Him? I promise you, you'll KNOW.

How do you need to "pray"? There's no need for formal words or a structured prayer. It's a relationship. You talk to Him in your words, your way. Awkward is great. Stumbling is great. Just talk to Him.

He already knows your life story. Your thoughts and story are an open book to God. He knows you better than you've ever known yourself. He loves you!

After you've talked it out with God, you get to start a new life. Your most important relationship from this point on will be with your Savior.

How do you prioritize this brand new relationship? The same way you would with a new baby or romantic partner. You spend lots of time with them—getting to know them, sharing yourself with them. You want to build a solid relationship with God that will last into eternity—because it will!

God gave us His love letter and instruction manual in the form of a Bible. If you don't already have one, you can find one in most hotel room nightstand drawers, in the library, at the dollar store, or as a free app on any phone or device.

To develop Christian community and learn more about the new love of your life, you can attend a church. Ask God to direct you to one. You can also watch Christian television or listen to ministry podcasts and Christian radio stations. Again, ask God to direct you.

Welcome to the family of God. You're LOVED!

"For ye are all the children of God by faith in Christ Jesus" (Galatians 3:26).

You also get to invite the Comforter, also known as the Holy Spirit, into your life. He gives us the power to heal and transform. When Jesus returned to heaven to be with His Father, He sent the Holy Spirit to live in us. The Holy Spirit fills us, gives us gifts, and empowers us.

Yes, you just ask Him. In your own words. We get to be in relationship with all three aspects of God: Father God who created us, the Son who died for our sins, and the Holy Spirit who lives in us.

Now that our hearts are focused on God, let's get started on our journey of being transformed by His perfect love.

Week 1

I AM
BRILLIANT

MOUNTAINS

When you look at a mountain, or even a photo of a mountain, what do you think? Are you intrigued? Do you want to explore it and climb to the top? From far away, it may look like climbing to the top of a mountain is a fairly easy task, but once you start climbing, it can quickly become apparent that getting to the top of most mountains takes much more effort and time than expected.

The climb up to the mountain peak can be challenging and filled with surprises. Do you have what it takes to make it to the top?

Will you get distracted? Will you get lost? Will you quit when the going gets rough?

In the Bible, there are several times where God calls men to go to the mountain top. Sometimes it was to test them, sometimes it was to get their attention, and sometimes it was to show them His glory. Even the Temple of the Lord in Jerusalem was built on top of a mountain!

In Genesis 22:1-3, God called Abraham to the mountain top to test him. He wanted to see if Abraham would be obedient and trust Him even when he didn't understand.

God used mountains to show His glory to Moses and to the Israelites:

> "So He said, 'Go forth and stand on the mountain before the Lord.' And behold, the Lord was passing by!" (1 Kings 19:11-13).

> "So it came about on the third day, when it was morning, that there were thunder and lightning flashes and a thick cloud upon the mountain and a very loud trumpet sound, so that all the people who were in the camp trembled. And Moses brought the people out of the camp to meet God, and they stood at the foot of the mountain. Now Mount Sinai was all in smoke because the Lord descended upon it in fire; and its smoke ascended like the smoke of a furnace, and the whole mountain quaked violently" (Exodus 19:16-19).

Jesus often prayed on mountain tops, and in Matthew 17:1-8, He was transfigured before some of His disciples. Later, Peter said:

> "For we did not follow cleverly devised tales when we made known to you the power and coming of our Lord Jesus Christ, but we were eyewitnesses of His majesty. For when He received honor and glory from God the Father, such an utterance as this was made to Him by the Majestic Glory, 'This is My beloved Son with whom I am well-pleased'— and we ourselves heard this utterance made from heaven when we were with Him on the holy mountain" (2 Peter 1:16-18).

God is waiting on the mountain top for you, wanting to show you His glory. He wants you to climb with Him to a place you can experience His presence and hear His voice more clearly.

God is ready. Are YOU ready to begin your mountain journey with Him?

IN CHRIST,

I AM BRILLIANT

I AM BOLD
I AM BRAVE
I AM BLESSED
I AM BELOVED

I AM
A SON OF A GOOD FATHER

AND AN
HEIR OF A GREAT KING

DAY 1

I AM BRILLIANT

And do not be conformed to this world, but be transformed by the renewing of your mind, that you may prove what is the good and acceptable and perfect will of God.
Romans 12:2 (NKJV)

It's transformation time! It is time to become the new you, the true you – the you that your Creator, King and Father had in mind when He created you both brilliantly and brilliant! It is time to say "NO" to this world and to being corrupted by and molded to its wrong ways. It is time to say "YES" to being transformed!

You may ask, "What does it mean to be transformed?" To be transformed means to be made into something new. Imagine yourself for a moment as a butterfly that is transformed from a crawling caterpillar to a colorful creature, no longer bound to the earth. You rise to float, flutter and fly into the heavens, bringing beauty and inspiration everywhere you go.

You may ask, "But how can I be transformed?" The Bible answers simply with "by renewing your mind." Your next question is likely, "How do I renew my mind?" We will go over that topic more in depth next week, but the simplest answer is: with the help of the Holy Spirit, train your mind to think like Jesus.

MEDITATION/JOURNAL

Think about today's Bible verse and ask the Holy Spirit to reveal to you what it means to be transformed by the renewing of your mind. Journal your thoughts.

_____

_____

_____

_____

_____

_____

_____

_____

_____

_____

_____

_____

_____

_____

_____

THE CHALLENGE

Memorize today's Scripture, Romans 12:2. Speak this verse over yourself every day this week saying, "I am no longer being conformed to this world, but I am being transformed by the renewing of my mind that I may prove what is the good, acceptable and perfect will of God."

THE PRAYER

Father, I choose to no longer be conformed to this world but instead to be transformed by the renewing of my mind. Because of what Jesus did for me, I know it is possible to have a brilliant mind and to be a new, glorious creation. Thank you! Holy Spirit, please train, teach and transform me by renewing my mind.

THE TRANSFORMATION

How has God transformed an area of your life through today's lesson?

IN CHRIST,

I AM BRILLIANT

I AM BOLD
I AM BRAVE
I AM BLESSED
I AM BELOVED

I AM
A SON OF A GOOD FATHER

AND AN
HEIR OF A GREAT KING

DAY 2

I AM BRILLIANT

Repent for the kingdom of Heaven is at hand.
Matthew 4:17

Renewing the mind begins with repentance. The word repent literally means to change your mind and go in a better direction. Jesus said, "Repent, for the kingdom of Heaven is at hand" (Matthew 4:17). Romans 8:6 says "to be carnally minded is death, but to be spiritually minded is life and peace." We are to renew our minds, our hearts and every part of our lives, because without repentance, we are locked into old "carnal" ways of thinking that lead us into darkness, destruction and—ultimately—death.

To be carnally minded is to be selfish. It means putting what you want before what God would want for you. The funny thing is, when we trust God and put His Kingdom and others first, we end up getting what we really need and want! The Bible says when we seek God's Kingdom and His righteousness first, all we really want and need are then ultimately given to us. He is a good father who wants what is ultimately best for his kids. If you have chosen Christ, then that includes you!

As you mature in your relationship with God, His purpose for your life will keep expanding. That's why it's important to keep renewing your mind and producing "fruits of repentance." It will be a daily choice as long as you are earth bound.

A wise person once said, "Sow a thought, and you reap an act; Sow an act, and you reap a habit; Sow a habit, and you reap a character; Sow a character, and you reap a destiny." When you repent of your sinful thoughts, actions and habits, then you are transformed by the changing and renewing of your mind. Your Heavenly Father has a good plan and destiny for your life because He is good and because He loves you. His destination for you is Heaven, but He also desires for you to be part of His Kingdom plan while you are on earth! When you repent and allow God to renew your mind and heart, He is able to use you to your fullest potential as an heir in His Kingdom.

MEDITATION/JOURNAL

Think about today's Bible verse and ask the Holy Spirit to reveal to you what it looks like to have Christ on the throne of your mind, heart and life. Journal your thoughts.

_____

_____

_____

_____

_____

_____

_____

_____

_____

_____

_____

_____

_____

_____

_____

_____

THE CHALLENGE

Look into your heart and repent of going your own selfish, carnal way. Choose to surrender to Christ and go His way. His Holy Spirit will go with you to be your helper. Choose to dethrone yourself and become His Heir by putting Christ on the throne of your mind, heart and life.

THE PRAYER

Father, I choose to make you King by putting You on the throne of my mind, heart and life. I trust you to help me walk your way which ultimately will lead me to life, peace and a heavenly destiny! Thank you for being my King and Good Father.

THE TRANSFORMATION

How has God transformed an area of your life through today's lesson?

IN CHRIST,

I AM BRILLIANT

I AM BOLD
I AM BRAVE
I AM BLESSED
I AM BELOVED

I AM
A SON OF A GOOD FATHER

AND AN
HEIR OF A GREAT KING

DAY 3

I AM BRILLIANT

Since you have heard about Jesus and have learned the truth that comes from Him, throw off your old sinful nature and your former way of life, which is corrupted by lust and deception. Instead, let the Spirit renew your mind, thoughts and attitudes. Put on your new nature, created to be like God—truly righteous and holy.
Ephesians 4:21-24 (NLT)

Jesus promised that He would guide you into all truth. To be of any use to the Kingdom, our minds must be transformed by His Truth. The Bible gives us a clue as to what transformation looks like in the story of Jesus's transfiguration. "And (Jesus) was transformed before them; and His countenance shone like the sun, and His garments became dazzling as brilliant as light" (Matthew 17:2).

The reality of Heaven radiated through Jesus, and He shone with incredible brilliance. The word *transformed* in that passage is the same word we find in the Bible verse we studied on day one, Romans 12:2. In a similar way, Jesus shone with Heaven's brilliance. It's not just that our thoughts are different; our way of thinking is transformed because we think Heaven's thoughts.

Let the Holy Spirit renew your mind through your thoughts and attitudes. Remember, you are a new creation with a new nature and a renewed mind created to be like God.

When you are transformed, you are brilliant!

MEDITATION/JOURNAL

Review the Eternal Heir Affirmation. How are they like the characteristics of God? Journal your thoughts.

_____

_____

_____

_____

_____

_____

_____

_____

_____

_____

_____

_____

_____

THE CHALLENGE

Think about the kind of person you believe God created you to be, and write out those characteristics. Then, speak those characteristics out loud using "I am" statements, such as "I am honest."

_____

THE PRAYER

Holy Spirit, reveal any lies I have believed about myself and replace those lies with your truth. Renew my mind, attitudes and thoughts. Make me a new creation. Make me like You.

_____

THE TRANSFORMATION

How has God transformed an area of your life through today's lesson?

IN CHRIST,

I AM BRILLIANT

I AM BOLD
I AM BRAVE
I AM BLESSED
I AM BELOVED

I AM
A SON OF A GOOD FATHER

AND AN
HEIR OF A GREAT KING

DAY 4

I AM BRILLIANT

For God has not given us the spirit of fear; but of power, of love, and of a sound mind.
2 Timothy 1:7

When you are ruled by fear instead of by your King, you are powerless, loveless and fearful. You are confused and find it difficult to determine God's delightful destiny for your life. Fear comes to the front when your mind is not in harmony with the mind of Christ. Even though you don't always know the outcome of your life, choose to trust your Good Father with the unknown, because it's not unknown to Him.

There is a battle that is being waged for control of your mind. You have a real enemy—Satan—and that enemy will use every weapon his twisted mind can conceive to attack your mind. He'll distract you with busyness, sin and even with noise. He'll seek to oppress you with fear, anxiety and even guilt over past mistakes. He will strive to keep your thoughts meditating on your fears, circumstances and yourself instead of on your God. Remember, what you meditate on, you magnify.

The good news is you are not alone in this battle! In fact, you have access to the mind of Christ, because if you have accepted Christ, He lives within you, and He will help you. His Holy Spirit and His help are only a prayer away. Your part is to call on the Holy Spirit, asking for Him to be your Counselor and to help you take every thought captive and evict any spirit of fear from your heart and mind.

MEDITATION/JOURNAL

Ask the Holy Spirit to reveal any place a spirit of fear lurks in the recesses of your mind or heart. Ask Him to give you strategies to equip you to be fearless. Journal your thoughts.

_____

_____

_____

_____

_____

_____

_____

_____

_____

_____

_____

_____

_____

_____

THE CHALLENGE

Starting today, decide to refuse fear—period. Instead, choose to take every thought captive to Christ. Choose to believe that you have a sound mind because you have invited a Spirit of love and power into your heart and mind.

THE PRAYER

Father, I praise You for giving me a spirit of power, love and a sound mind. I choose to be obedient to the Holy Spirit, and I choose to exercise self-control by taking captive every thought. Help me choose to be fearless and no longer fearful. I thank You that I will win the battle for my mind by rejecting fearful thoughts and focusing on what is good, excellent and praiseworthy. I will meditate only on what I want magnified.

THE TRANSFORMATION

How has God transformed an area of your life through today's lesson?

IN CHRIST,

I AM BRILLIANT

I AM BOLD
I AM BRAVE
I AM BLESSED
I AM BELOVED

I AM
A SON OF A GOOD FATHER

AND AN
HEIR OF A GREAT KING

DAY 5

I AM BRILLIANT

As a person thinks in their heart, so that is who they are.
Proverbs 23:7

Renewing your mind does not just mean to think different thoughts. It means to change what you really believe about yourself, about God and—well, everything! A person is literally what they think and believe in their mind and heart. A plant grows up from a seed; in the same way, who you are springs up from the hidden seeds that you nurture in your heart and mind. Sometimes those are good, and sometimes not so much!

A noble and Godly character is not magically achieved. It is the result of both natural and supernatural processes. It is achieved by your choice to renew your mind daily and even moment by moment. But you also have to surrender to the Holy Spirit, who then supernaturally transforms your mind to that of the mind of Christ—thinking His thoughts about you and those around you.

A heart that seeks to love God is a heart that can come to know who He is. This brings a mind change that enables you to see reality from His perspective.

It is true that you become what you behold. If you behold brilliant thoughts in your mind, you will become brilliant. If you behold peaceful thoughts, you will become peaceful. If you behold the thoughts of God expressed in the Bible, you will become Godly. That is why it is good to memorize Scripture verses. Sadly, the opposite is true. As you behold negative and dark thoughts, you are more likely, over time, to become negative and dark. The Bible counsels us to guard our hearts above all else, because from the heart flows the true issues of life (Proverbs 4:23). So, choose wisely what thoughts you allow in your mind and heart, because your choices will affect the rest of your life.

MEDITATION/JOURNAL

Think about today's Bible verse, and ask the Holy Spirit to help you discipline yourself to believe and behold what you want to become. Journal your thoughts.

_____

_____

_____

_____

_____

_____

_____

_____

_____

_____

_____

_____

_____

_____

_____

_____

_____

THE CHALLENGE

Every hour today, stop and ask yourself what it is you are thinking. Every day over the next month, stop at least once and think about your thoughts. If your thoughts are not God thoughts, simply replace them with ones that are!

THE PRAYER

Father, help me today and every day to believe and behold in my heart what and who you want me to become.

THE TRANSFORMATION

How has God transformed an area of your life through today's lesson?

IN CHRIST,

I AM BRILLIANT

I AM BOLD
I AM BRAVE
I AM BLESSED
I AM BELOVED

I AM
A SON OF A GOOD FATHER

AND AN
HEIR OF A GREAT KING

DAY 6

I AM BRILLIANT

Who has known the mind of the Lord so as to instruct him?
But we have the mind of Christ.
1 Corinthians 2:16

You have the mind of Christ because His Spirit and Kingdom are within you. You have access to His wisdom, His brilliance and His light. Whatever problems you face, pray for His face to shine upon and within you. He holds heavenly answers to life's problems. If you are facing situations with unresolved conflict or seeming impossibilities, ask Him to show you His perspective. He promised if we seek, we will find. His word tells us to "call upon me and I will answer and tell you great and unsearchable things you do not know" (Jeremiah 33:3).

Jesus' life and ministry revealed the Father's will, and He fulfilled that will through the anointing of the Holy Spirit. Today you see that the Holy Spirit lives in you. The Holy Spirit is conforming you to the image of Christ and transforming your mind as a son of God called to reveal the will of the Father. You are called not only to imitate Christ but to have the mind of Christ and have his light and his Kingdom alive within you. God did not say, "Rise and Reflect," but, "Rise and Shine!" (Isaiah 60:1). Jesus said, "You are the light of the world. Let your light so shine before men that they may see your good works and give glory to God."

So, believe you are brilliant. Believe in the Light within you. Rise and shine for the glory of God!

MEDITATION/JOURNAL

Think about today's Bible verse, and ask the Holy Spirit to reveal to you what it means to be transformed by the renewing of your mind. Journal your thoughts.

_____

_____

_____

_____

_____

_____

_____

_____

_____

_____

_____

_____

_____

_____

THE CHALLENGE

Take some time today to thank the Holy Spirit for His presence in your life. Try talking less in your prayer time, listening and allowing the Holy Spirit speak to you. Ask Him to reveal the mind of Christ and His thoughts to you.

THE PRAYER

Father, I choose to no longer be conformed to this world but instead to be transformed by the renewing of my mind. Thank you that because of what Jesus did for me, it is possible to have a brilliant mind and to be a new, glorious creation! Holy Spirit, please train, teach and transform me by renewing my mind.

THE TRANSFORMATION

How has God transformed an area of your life through today's lesson?

IN CHRIST,

I AM BRILLIANT

I AM BOLD
I AM BRAVE
I AM BLESSED
I AM BELOVED

I AM
A SON OF A GOOD FATHER

AND AN
HEIR OF A GREAT KING

DAY 7

I AM BRILLIANT

Rejoice in the Lord always. Again I will say, rejoice! Let your gentleness be known to all men. The Lord is at hand. Be anxious for nothing, but in everything by prayer and supplication, with thanksgiving, make your requests known to God; and the peace of God, which surpasses all understanding, will guard your hearts and mind through Christ Jesus. Finally, brethren, whatever things are true, whatever things are noble, whatever things are just, whatever things are pure, whatever things are lovely, whatever things are of good report, if there is any virtue and if there is anything praiseworthy—meditate on these things. The things which you learned and received and heard and saw in me, these do, and the God of peace will be with you.
Philippians 4:4-9 (NKJV)

An important part of being transformed by the renewing of your mind is filling up your mind and overflowing your heart with prayer. If you want to be joyful, then rejoice even when there seems to be no reason for it at all. If you want peace, then fill your mind with prayer. Peace pervades where prayer and praise are present. As these verses also show us, thanksgiving is important in keeping the soil of our minds fertile. If you want to think and be great, be grateful.

What you meditate on you magnify. What you behold you become. You are what you believe in your heart. That is why it is of ultimate importance that you think God thoughts. What are the God thoughts you should think about? Whatever is "true, honorable, right, pure, lovely, of good report, excellent and praiseworthy."

Few people actually think about what they are thinking about. With the busyness of life, it is easy to be unaware of the quality of your thoughts. A vital part of transformation is not only choosing to think about your own thoughts, but also to focus your mind on God thoughts. To learn what God might think, we must learn who God is. We know from God's Word that God is Love, and He is Good, Joyful, Faithful, Kind, Merciful, Gracious, Patient, Creative, and so much more. Choose to think transforming thoughts that reflect His character, goodness and glory. Be transformed by thinking God thoughts!

MEDITATION/JOURNAL

Think about today's Bible verse, and ask the Holy Spirit to help you put into practice all you are learning. Journal your thoughts.

_____

_____

_____

_____

_____

_____

_____

_____

_____

_____

_____

_____

_____

_____

_____

_____

THE CHALLENGE

Ask the Holy Spirit to reveal something wonderful about who He is and His gracious thoughts towards you.

_____

THE PRAYER

Father, I choose to rejoice, pray and be thankful. I choose to think on "whatever is true, whatever is honorable, whatever is right, whatever is pure, whatever is lovely, whatever is of good repute, if there is any excellence and if anything worthy of praise." Guard my heart and mind, and grant me peace. Help me put into practice all that I am learning.

_____

THE TRANSFORMATION

How has God transformed an area of your life through today's lesson?

Week 2

I AM
BOLD

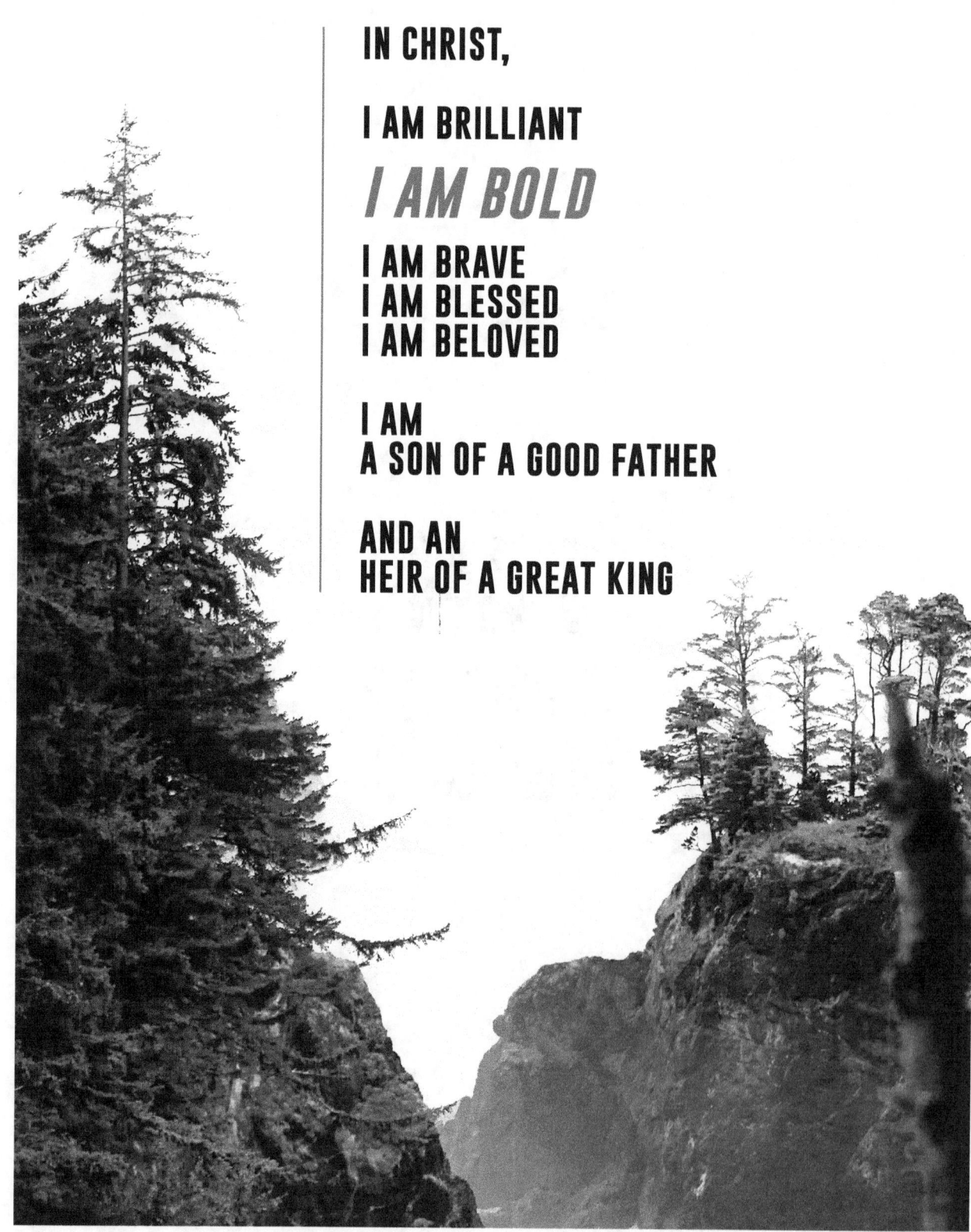

IN CHRIST,

I AM BRILLIANT

I AM BOLD

I AM BRAVE
I AM BLESSED
I AM BELOVED

I AM
A SON OF A GOOD FATHER

AND AN
HEIR OF A GREAT KING

DAY 8

I AM BOLD

*Have I not commanded you? Be strong and courageous. Do not be afraid, and do not
be discouraged, for the Lord your God will be with you wherever you go."*
Joshua 1:9 (NIV)

Did you know that the Lord wants you to be bold? What do you think of when you think of
boldness? Someone fearless? Someone who does dangerous things? There is a difference between
worldly boldness and the kind of boldness the Lord calls us to walk in. Worldly boldness may
look like just saying whatever is on your mind and not caring what others think, or doing dangerous or risky things that could get us into trouble. Worldly boldness might give us more rank
with our "friends" when we seem unafraid to choose behaviors that may hurt others. It's making
wrong choices for the sake of looking strong or courageous. In reality, worldly boldness is based
on fear, because we act "bold" to prove to others that we aren't afraid or weak.

On the other hand, Godly boldness is doing the right thing in the Lord's eyes and not fearing the
consequences. It's doing what the Bible says and speaking the truth because we want to glorify
God, even though we might be afraid. When God says He wants us to be bold, He wants us to
trust Him and seek His protection through life's trials, temptations and difficulties. This kind of
boldness lets go of fear and hands all control over to our God; it is based on trust in Him. When
we are bold in the Lord, we are saying, "I may not know what is going to happen, or what the end
result will be, but I trust that God will take care of me."

Your Father wants you to be bold, but not because of your own strength when you stand up for
yourself or protect yourself. Godly boldness comes because you know that He is by your side
wherever you go. He wants you to trust Him more than you trust yourself, and He wants you to
seek Him in every situation. He wants you to come to Him in your time of need and ask for His
help!

MEDITATION/JOURNAL

Think about different situations where you have felt the need to be in control and have acted in "worldly boldness." Then think how you could have acted in Godly boldness instead. How would that have changed your situation? Journal your thoughts.

_____

_____

_____

_____

_____

_____

_____

_____

_____

_____

_____

_____

_____

THE CHALLENGE

Memorize today's Scripture, Joshua 1:9. Speak this scripture over yourself every day this week like this, "I am strong and courageous. I will not be dismayed , for the Lord my God is with me wherever I go."

THE PRAYER

Father, help me to trust you and walk in Godly boldness. Help me to seek you in all situations where I feel the need to stand up for myself or protect myself. Show me how to rely on your protection.

THE TRANSFORMATION

How has God transformed an area of your life through today's lesson?

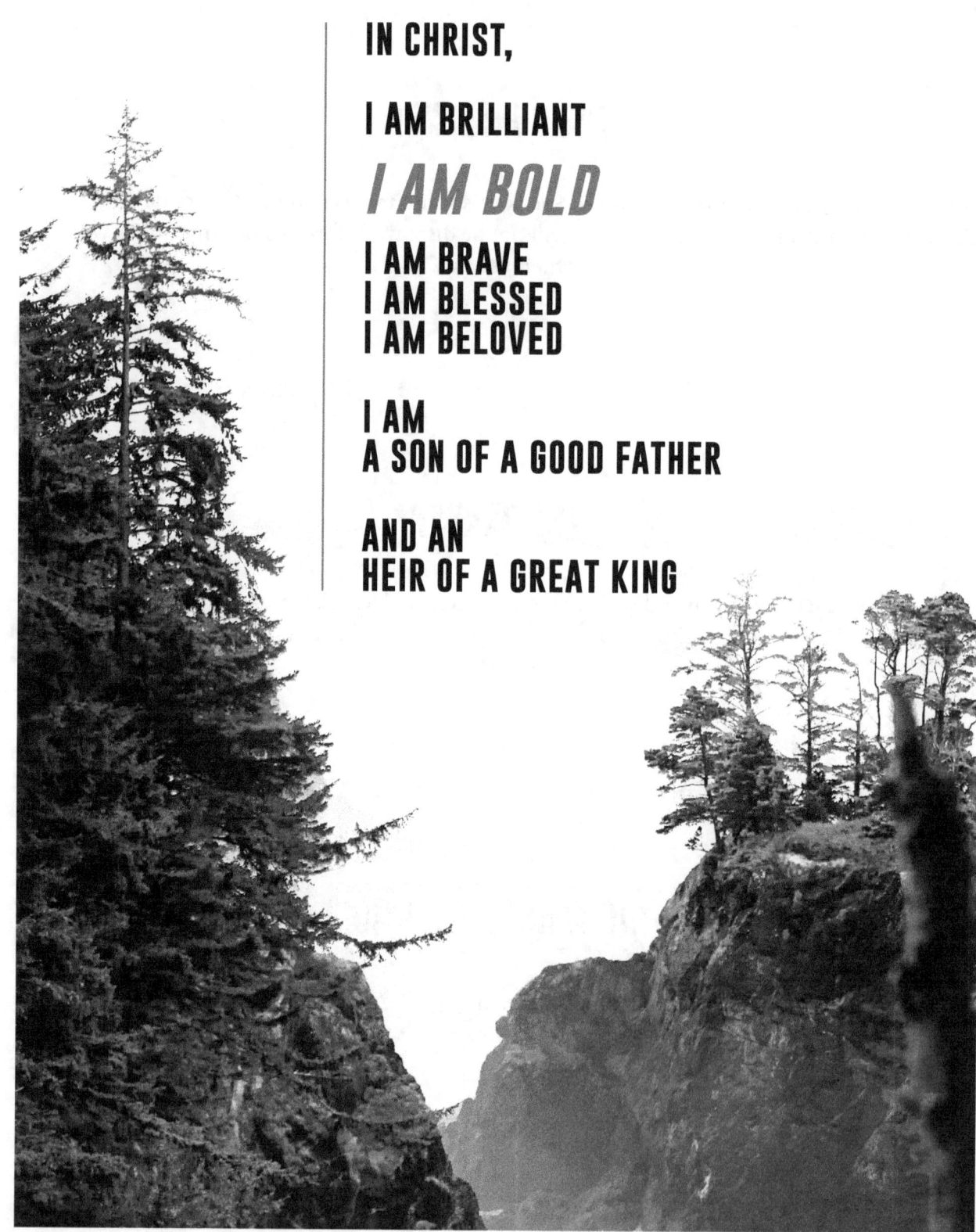

IN CHRIST,

I AM BRILLIANT

I AM BOLD

I AM BRAVE
I AM BLESSED
I AM BELOVED

I AM
A SON OF A GOOD FATHER

AND AN
HEIR OF A GREAT KING

DAY 9

I AM BOLD

Be alert and of sober mind. Your enemy the devil prowls around like
a roaring lion looking for someone to devour.
1 Peter 5:8 (NIV)

To be bold we must have a sober mind. To be sober-minded means that we are not only clear from addictive substances and behaviors, such as drugs, alcohol, fornication, or pornography, but it also means that we recognize the obstacles of sin that the enemy places in our way to cloud our view and distract us from doing what is right. Being of sober mind means we understand that God has a higher calling for our life – a path that He has set before us – and that if we choose that path, we will experience many blessings along the way. We will be walking in His plan for us and fulfilling the calling that He has chosen for us.

This does not mean we won't have problems, but if we are of sober mind, we will be able to see the schemes of the enemy when he is trying to ensnare us, and we can choose to not fall into the trap! We can see the way out of those snares because we are not distracted.

The way we stay sober minded is by seeking God daily through reading His word and by prayer. The word says that we should "Rejoice always, pray continually, give thanks in all circumstances; for this is God's will for you in Christ Jesus"(1 Thessalonians 5:16-18 NIV).

It is also wise to find a family of believers and Godly mentors who can help you see things clearly, especially when you are a new believer. But even as you grow in the word, the Lord often uses other people to speak into our lives and help keep us accountable.

MEDITATION/JOURNAL

Think about ways the enemy is consistently trying to trap you with sin patterns that you would like to break free from. Ask the Lord to show you the schemes of the enemy and how to overcome them. Journal your thoughts.

_____

_____

_____

_____

_____

_____

_____

_____

_____

_____

_____

_____

_____

THE CHALLENGE

Every day this week, first thing in the morning, look at yourself in the mirror and say, "In Christ I am brilliant, and I am bold!"

THE PRAYER

Lord Jesus, help me understand the ways the enemy is trying to devour me. Lord, give me a sober mind so that I can think clearly when the enemy tries to trick me, and so that I can choose to do right in your eyes. Help me walk in the calling you have for my life. Help my mind to turn away from the things of this world and towards you.

THE TRANSFORMATION

How has God transformed an area of your life through today's lesson?

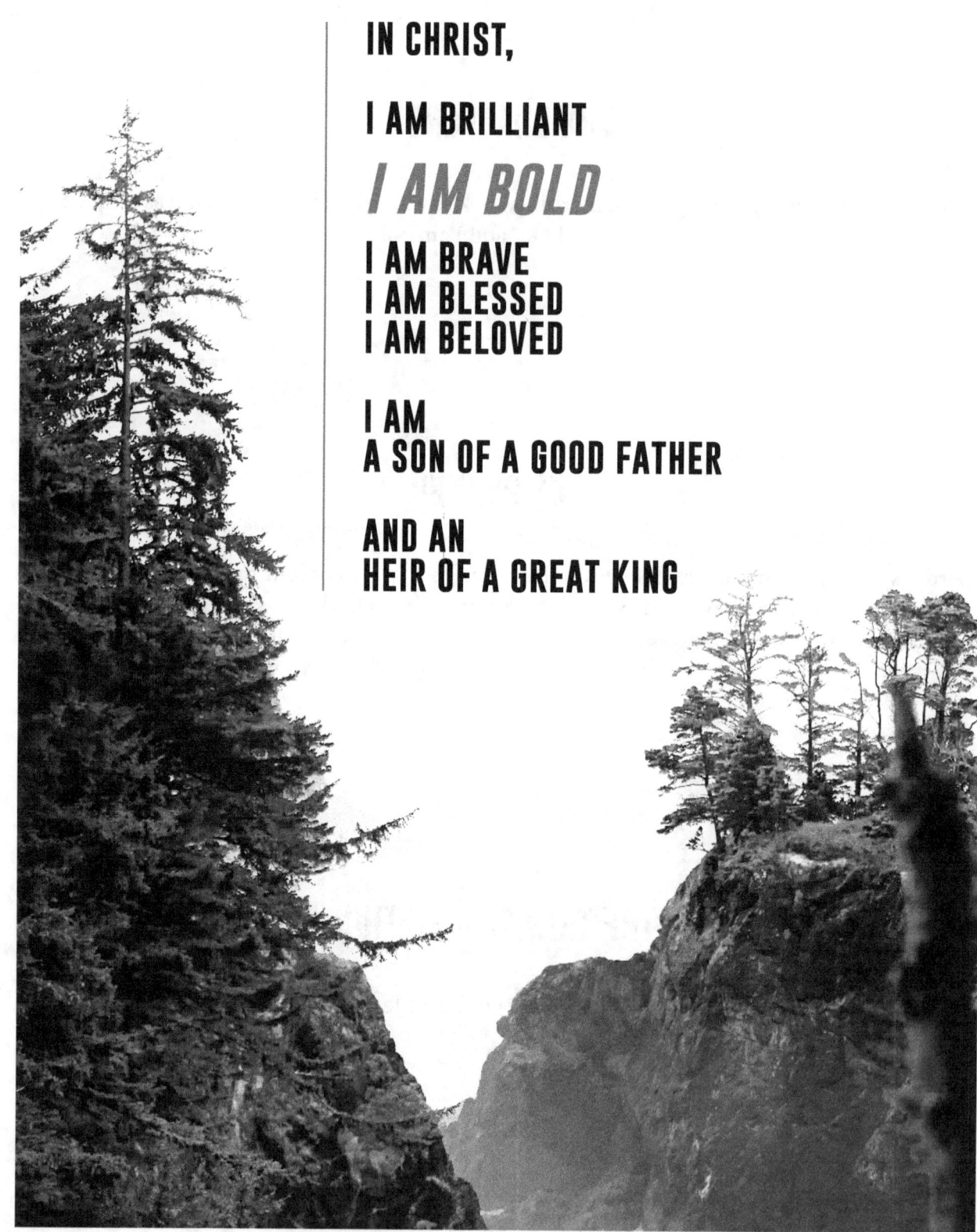

IN CHRIST,

I AM BRILLIANT

I AM BOLD

I AM BRAVE
I AM BLESSED
I AM BELOVED

I AM
A SON OF A GOOD FATHER

AND AN
HEIR OF A GREAT KING

DAY 10

I AM BOLD

So now, little children, remain in Him, so that when He appears we may have boldness and not be ashamed before Him at His coming.
1 John 2:28 (NIV)

We've all made mistakes in life, and we've all experienced shame. Sometimes it's because of something we have done ourselves, sometimes it's something someone has done to us, and sometimes it's just because of our circumstances. One awesome thing about your Father in Heaven is that when we accept Him as our Lord and Savior, we become a new creation in Him. The old things, including our shame, have passed away, and we are made new. "This means that anyone who belongs to Christ has become a new person. The old life is gone; a new life has begun!" (2 Corinthians 5:17).

When you become a new Christian, you can trust that the Lord sees you and is pleased with you. The Bible says that He removes our sins away from us as far as the East is from the West! That means He does not even remember our sin. It's gone from us. But often times, the enemy tries to remind us about what we did or what was done to us. When you hear a nagging voice telling you to "remember that you (fill in the blank)," or "remember when(fill in the blank)," you know this is from the enemy. Just start thanking God that He made you a new creation and that you are not that person anymore! Live in Christ by continually talking with him and reading His word. That will drown out the voice of the enemy!

Shame and conviction are not the same. If you are feeling like you should not have done something, and you have not repented (turned away from) a certain sin, that is the Holy Spirit prompting you to repent. You should ask the Lord to forgive you, and pray about asking the person you hurt for forgiveness, and then turn away from that sin. When you are cut to the heart about a situation that occurred, that's conviction. The voice of conviction sounds like, "I think I hurt this person, so I really should apologize." Shame says, "You are no good—look what you did! You will never overcome this. You will always be_____." As you grow in the Lord, you will learn to know which voice is the Lord and which one is the enemy. You can walk in the confidence that God loves you, doesn't shame you, and that He is a God of creation who can create a new heart in you.

MEDITATION/JOURNAL

Ask the Lord to show you how to abide, or live, in Him. Ask Him to show you the difference between conviction and shame. Journal your thoughts.

_____

_____

_____

_____

_____

_____

_____

_____

_____

_____

_____

_____

_____

_____

_____

THE CHALLENGE

Write a list of things that make you feel ashamed, and prayerfully take them to the Lord, asking Him for forgiveness or healing for those things. Ask Him to remove them from you as far as the East is from the West.

THE PRAYER

Lord, help me to to abide in you. Show me how to do this daily so that I can be confident in your love for me. Show me where I need to repent, and then help me to move on and not listen to the voice of shame anymore.

THE TRANSFORMATION

How has God transformed an area of your life through today's lesson?

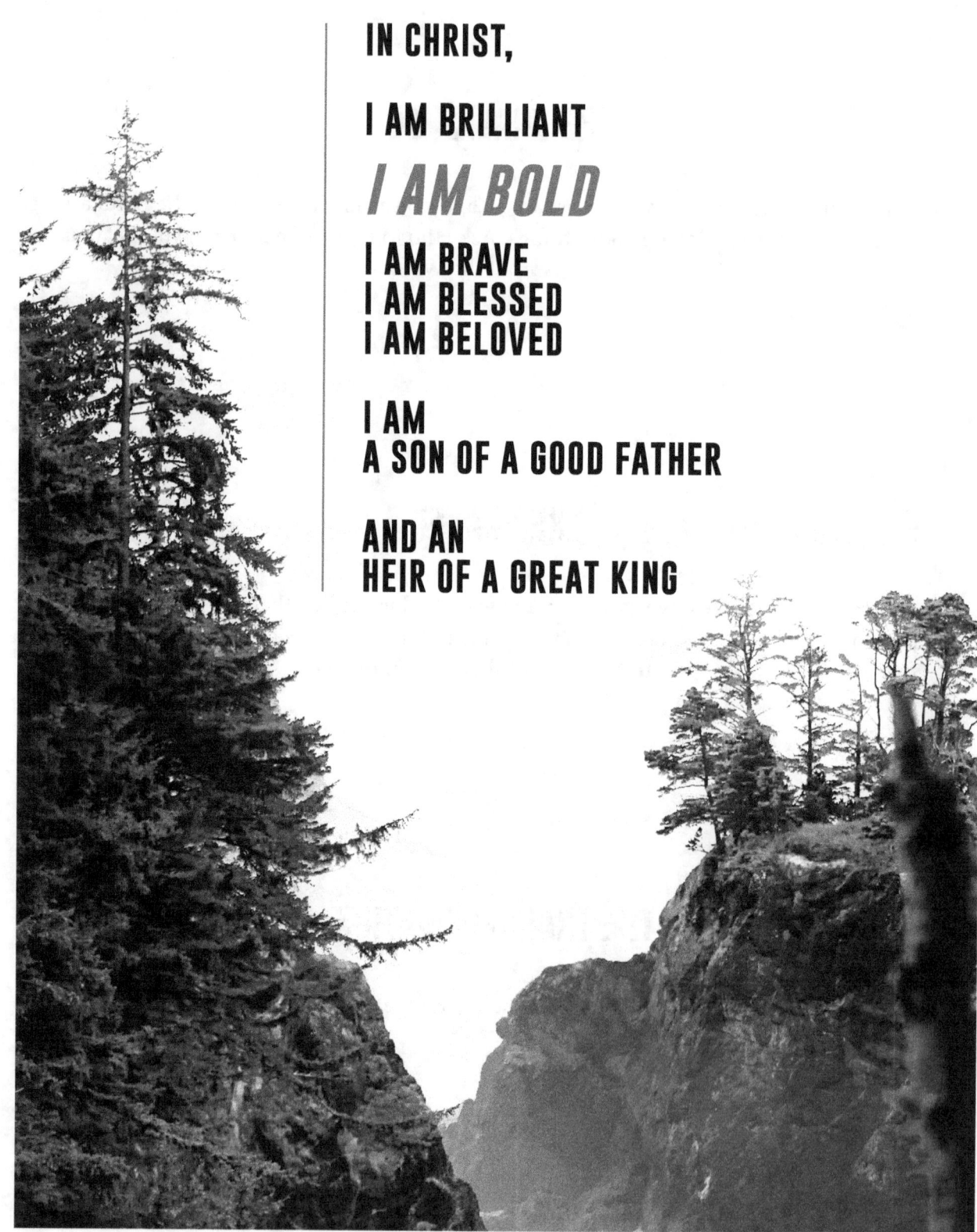

IN CHRIST,

I AM BRILLIANT

I AM BOLD

I AM BRAVE
I AM BLESSED
I AM BELOVED

I AM
A SON OF A GOOD FATHER

AND AN
HEIR OF A GREAT KING

DAY 11

I AM BOLD

Let us approach the throne of grace with boldness, so that we may receive mercy and find grace to help us at the proper time.
Hebrews 4:16

So many times, we think that once we are saved, we will not have any more problems. We believe that all we have to do is pray, and all our problems will be solved right away. This is not true. Jesus is not a magic genie in a bottle. Sometimes we go through tests and trials, and the Bible even says we will have many troubles in this life. But, trials are opportunities for us to grow closer to the Father and not allow ourselves to be angry, hurt, impatient, aggravated and just give up on our relationship with God because we feel like He didn't come through, or that He abandoned us.

When times are the most difficult, we should be storming heaven with our prayers and reading His word even more. That's the time to approach His throne in boldness through our heartfelt prayers. When we turn to Him during our toughest hour, that is when He has the most room to work miracles in our lives. That's when He turns our test into a testimony. When we have made it through and proved to be faithful through the trial, then we can help someone else who is going through the same situation and point them to Christ.

As long as the enemy is out to kill, steal and destroy, we will have problems, but the Lord promises He is working everything for our good. It may not be in our timing, and we may wait days, months, even years to see our answered prayers, but we can not give up. We must ask the Lord to give us the mercy and grace to make it through the situation. We know He will do that, because the word says He will help us at the proper time.

Remember that Jesus suffered on earth for our sins, and He experienced temptation and even death without sinning. He knows what we go through and has shown us the way to walk through suffering without sinning and without turning away from our Heavenly Father.

MEDITATION/JOURNAL

When you are going through rough times, ask the Holy Spirit to remind you that God is always on time. Ask Him to give you the boldness you need to continually go before God's throne in prayer, even when it seems hopeless. Journal your thoughts.

_____

_____

_____

_____

_____

_____

_____

_____

_____

_____

_____

_____

_____

_____

_____

THE CHALLENGE

Make a decision today to trust God's timing, even when things get hard and you feel like He isn't answering you. Trust that He is working everything for your good, even if you can't see it right away.

THE PRAYER

Father, thank you that you know my every need and that you want to give me grace and mercy in difficult times. Thank you that you sent your son Jesus to experience the same things I am going through and that He went through those things so that He might give me Eternal Life through His suffering and death. Help me to remember to come to you in times of trouble.

THE TRANSFORMATION

How has God transformed an area of your life through today's lesson?

IN CHRIST,

I AM BRILLIANT

I AM BOLD

I AM BRAVE
I AM BLESSED
I AM BELOVED

I AM
A SON OF A GOOD FATHER

AND AN
HEIR OF A GREAT KING

DAY 12

I AM BOLD

This is the confidence we have in approaching God:
that if we ask anything according to his will, he hears us.
1 John 5:14 (NKJV)

The Lord knows everything we need before we even ask. The Bible says He knows every hair on our head, and not one sparrow falls to the ground without Him knowing (Luke 12:7). But He still wants us to come to Him and ask when we are in need. Why? Because He is a gentle and loving Father. He will not force Himself on us, and He wants us to come to Him so that it is a mutual, loving relationship.

Notice that the scripture above says that we can ask anything of our Father and He hears us. We can be confident, or bold, about asking anything. Don't be afraid to ask the Lord for what you need! The word says that if we ask according to His will, He hears us. That doesn't mean we will automatically get what we want. Sometimes His will is to not give us what we are asking. This is because He sees and knows all things; we have to trust that He knows what is best for us. It could be that not giving us what we want is actually protecting us. Or there may be someone the Lord wants us to meet so we can help them out, and in order to do so, we need to take the path He chose for us rather than answer our prayer. Our boldness or confidence comes into play when we can sit tight and wait for an answer, and trust that God has a good reason for it if the answer doesn't come the way we thought it should.

Isaiah 22:22 says that what He opens no one can shut, and what he shuts no one can open. This is a great scripture to keep in mind, as sometimes the Lord closes doors in our lives, and sometimes He opens new doors for our safety and for our good. Do you trust the Lord to do what is best for you? Do you believe that He knows your every need and that He has your best interest at heart?

MEDITATION/JOURNAL

Think about some areas in your life that you have been wanting to go a certain way. Now give those areas of your life over to the Lord, and ask Him to do His will in your life in those areas. Journal your thoughts.

_____

_____

_____

_____

_____

_____

_____

_____

_____

_____

_____

_____

_____

_____

THE CHALLENGE

Think of some challenges you are facing right now. Go to the Lord and ask Him to work in your favor. Ask that He would open the doors He would like you to go through and close the ones He does not. Now trust Him to show you the way that is best for you.

THE PRAYER

Holy Spirit, help me believe God and trust Him patiently with my life. I pray that you would show me the doors you would like me to go through and close the ones you do not want me to go through.

THE TRANSFORMATION

How has God transformed an area of your life through today's lesson?

IN CHRIST,

I AM BRILLIANT

I AM BOLD

I AM BRAVE
I AM BLESSED
I AM BELOVED

I AM
A SON OF A GOOD FATHER

AND AN
HEIR OF A GREAT KING

DAY 13

I AM BOLD

Finally, be strong in the Lord and in his mighty power. Put on the full armor of God, so that you can take your stand against the devil's schemes. For our struggle is not against flesh and blood, but against the rulers, against the authorities, against the powers of this dark world and against the spiritual forces of evil in the heavenly realms. Therefore put on the full armor of God, so that when the day of evil comes, you may be able to stand your ground.
Ephesians 6:10 (NIV)

The Bible gives clear directions on how to defeat the enemy. It even tells us who our enemy is! A lot of times we find it hard to see past the people we are dealing with here on earth to the real enemy lurking behind them causing all kinds of trouble for us and them. The Bible is clear that we are not fighting people; we are fighting a spiritual battle. But the good news is that our Father doesn't leave us without a way to fight, even against an enemy we cannot see with our own eyes, AND He gives us HIS power to be strong, bold, and to overcome.

When we are dealing with someone who seems to be causing us problems, we need to take a moment to realize that it may actually be the enemy scheming against us and using that person as a tool. When we do that, we are already walking in the power of the Almighty! Half the battle is already won when we know the opposition's battle plan. The next step is to seek the Lord on how He would have us handle each situation. Sometimes we have to walk away and just pray, sometimes we have to talk it out with the person we are dealing with, or pray with that person. Sometimes we are called to love someone even when they are busy hurting us because we understand that it is not them we are fighting. And sometimes we are called to just simply stand. It takes a lot of courage to stand in the face of our enemy and even more courage to stand in the face of our friends when they are doing wrong because we fear being rejected or that we might lose their friendship. Sometimes when we stand for what is right, it feels like we are all alone. But take heart! The Lord is always with us, and He is the best friend we can ever have. He will be there when no one else is. And, in the end, when it comes time to spend eternity somewhere, He is all that will matter!

So be bold, and stand firm in the things of the Lord. Be courageous, be different, and let the Lord be your armor and protection in the battle!

MEDITATION/JOURNAL

Think about today's scripture throughout the day. Remember that others may be acting out of their own pain and suffering, and that the enemy might be causing people to react in certain ways. Walk in love, knowing you are not fighting people, and then take the time to pray for that person to see the truth, too. Journal your thoughts.

_____

_____

_____

_____

_____

_____

_____

_____

_____

_____

_____

_____

_____

_____

THE CHALLENGE

Practice letting the Lord be your armor. Ask Him to show you through the Holy Spirit what you are truly fighting against. Anytime you have an issue with someone today, ask the Lord to reveal the true enemy in the situation so that you can forgive the person you are dealing with.

THE PRAYER

Father, thank you that you are fighting the battle for us and your armor will protect and defend us. Lord, I ask that you would help me to see when I am fighting the schemes of the enemy. Remind me it is not the people around me that I should be fighting. Help me to fight in prayer, Lord!

THE TRANSFORMATION

How has God transformed an area of your life through today's lesson?

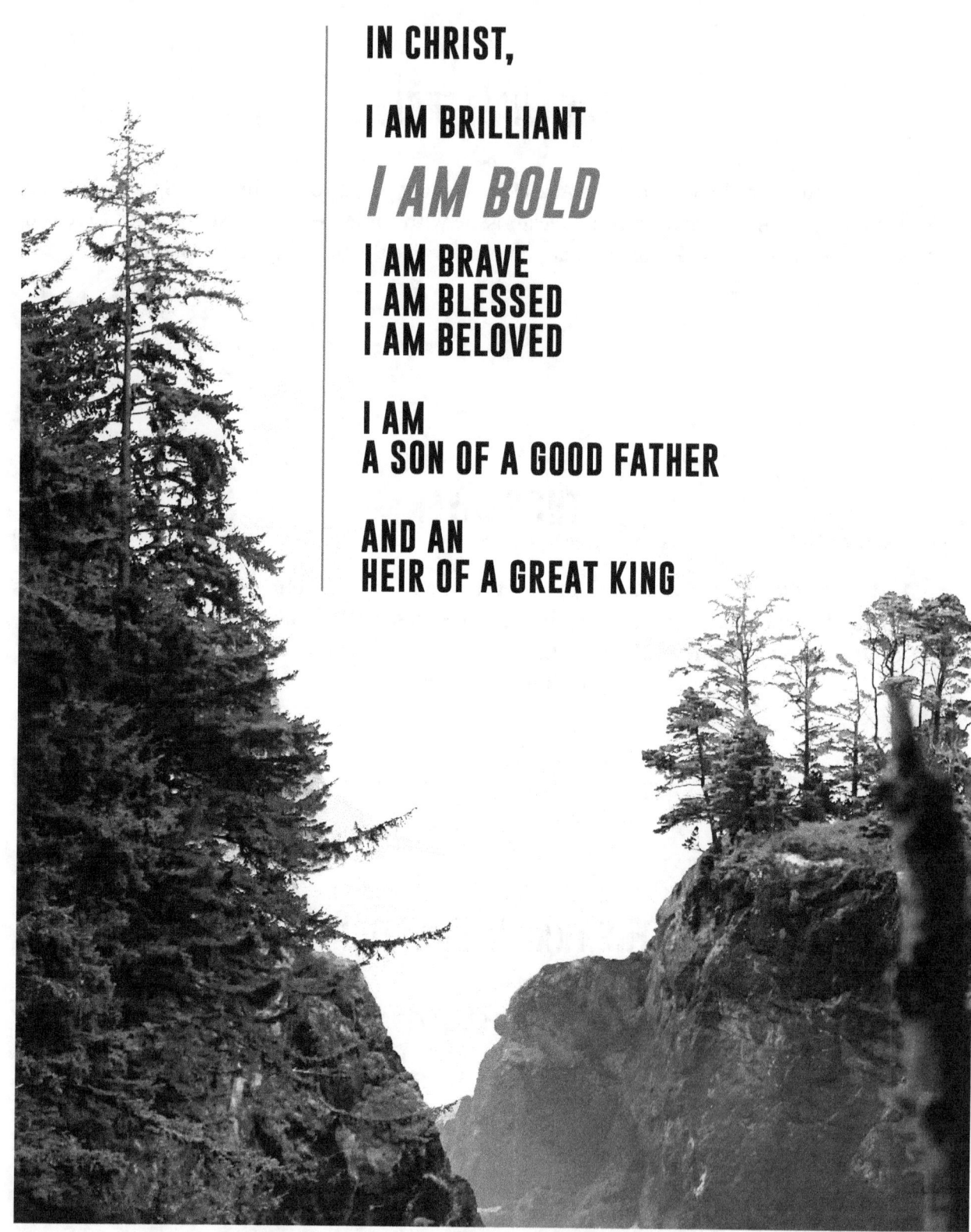

IN CHRIST,

I AM BRILLIANT

I AM BOLD

I AM BRAVE
I AM BLESSED
I AM BELOVED

I AM
A SON OF A GOOD FATHER

AND AN
HEIR OF A GREAT KING

DAY 14

I AM BOLD

Stand firm then, with the belt of truth buckled around your waist, with the breastplate of righteousness in place, and with your feet fitted with the readiness that comes from the gospel of peace. In addition to all this, take up the shield of faith, with which you can extinguish all the flaming arrows of the evil one. Take the helmet of salvation and the sword of the Spirit, which is the word of God.
Ephesian 6:14 (NIV)

True boldness is doing what is right in the face of evil, no matter the consequences. It's having the courage to take up your battle armor and face the flaming arrows of the enemy, knowing that what you are fighting for is more important than the loss of your own life. And when you take up the armor of God, you are, in a way, dying. You are dying to yourself and your old ways, because you are saying, "I choose to be different than I have been in the past." True boldness is choosing truth over deceiving. It's choosing to be righteous instead of falling back into old sin patterns. It's choosing to be ready in all seasons to be a carrier of peace instead of sowing discord or hurting others. It's choosing to have faith that the Lord will protect you, knowing that you do not have to always defend yourself. He will fight your battles and will extinguish the enemy's flaming arrows that are being thrown at you. True boldness is choosing to walk out your salvation by learning to trust the Father with your very life, and understanding that if He has saved you from eternal death, He will save you from harm here on earth. It's choosing to pick up the sword of the Spirit to fight each battle. The word of God, the Bible, is your sword!

Whenever you feel like you are in a battle, read the word of God! The Bible says that it is active and living, and when you need to fight in the spirit realm, read scripture out loud and pray the scriptures over yourself. This is your super power to fight off the enemy and to win the battle! The word of God cuts through the lies of the enemy by exposing them, and it also breaks the power of the enemy. The Bible says that the power of life and death is in the tongue, so when we speak the word of God or pray out loud, we have the power to destroy the works of the enemy through the power of God's word!

When we put on His armor every morning, we can have the boldness of God!

MEDITATION/JOURNAL

Think about the battle you are in right now. Ask the Lord to fight the battle, and imagine yourself wearing His armor of honesty, righteousness, peace, and faithfulness. Find a scripture that you can speak out loud today when things get hard. Journal your thoughts.

_____

_____

_____

_____

_____

_____

_____

_____

_____

_____

_____

_____

_____

_____

THE CHALLENGE

Put on your full armor today, and see how you can walk in peace as the Lord protects you and helps you.

THE PRAYER

Lord, thank you for giving me the belt of truth today, and for giving me a breastplate of righteousness as I walk through my day. Thank you for giving me shoes that are ready to carry the gospel of peace wherever I go. Thank you for the shield of faith you have given me to protect from the flaming arrows of the enemy. Thank you for protecting my mind with the helmet of salvation, and thank you for giving me your word to use as my sword to fight off the enemy!

THE TRANSFORMATION

How has God transformed an area of your life through today's lesson?

Week 3

I AM
BRAVE

IN CHRIST,

I AM BRILLIANT
I AM BOLD

I AM BRAVE

I AM BLESSED
I AM BELOVED

I AM
A SON OF A GOOD FATHER

AND AN
HEIR OF A GREAT KING

DAY 15

I AM BRAVE

Be strong and courageous. Do not be afraid or terrified because of them, for the Lord
your God goes with you; He will never leave you nor forsake you.
Deuteronomy 31:6 (NIV)

Your Father and King gives a clear command to be brave. We don't have to be afraid because He himself goes with us and promises to remain with us. What does it actually mean to be brave and courageous? It does not mean to be without any feelings of fear. It means to hold fast to your beliefs and your course of action regardless of the opposition, and no matter how formidable the foe.

In 1883, before he became president, Theodore Roosevelt embarked on a trip by himself to the badlands of North Dakota, where he encountered many bandits, bears, and situations that would have caused fear in the hearts of almost anyone. Roosevelt said what he learned from that experience was that in acting as if he had no fear, despite his feelings, he became fearless.

It's possible for you to be brave because your Good Father would not command you to do something that's impossible or unnecessary. Today's verse tells us we should not fear because God is with us and will not leave us. God commanded us to refuse fear 365 times in scripture; that's one time for every day of the year! Why did He remind us not to fear so many times? Because when we fear, we are actually agreeing with fear and not trusting God. When we choose to be brave, it is an act of faith in the power and goodness of God.

MEDITATION/JOURNAL

Think about today's Bible verse, and ask the Holy Spirit to reveal to you what it means to be transformed by being brave. Journal your thoughts.

_____

_____

_____

_____

_____

_____

_____

_____

_____

_____

_____

_____

_____

_____

THE CHALLENGE

Memorize today's Scripture, Deuteronomy 31:6. Speak this Scripture over yourself every day this week. For example, "I am strong and courageous. I am not afraid, for the Lord my God goes with me; He will never leave me or forsake me."

THE PRAYER

Father, I choose to be brave and courageous even when I experience feelings of fear. Help me to make courageous choices by trusting You.

THE TRANSFORMATION

How has God transformed an area of your life through today's lesson?

IN CHRIST,

I AM BRILLIANT
I AM BOLD

I AM BRAVE

I AM BLESSED
I AM BELOVED

I AM
A SON OF A GOOD FATHER

AND AN
HEIR OF A GREAT KING

DAY 16

I AM BRAVE

The angel of the LORD appeared to him and said to him,
"The LORD is with you, O valiant, brave warrior."
Judges 6:12

In the verse above, God called Gideon a "valiant, brave warrior" even while he was cowardly hiding to avoid a battle. Gideon certainly was not acting brave at the time. After God's encouragement, Gideon truly did become a "valiant, brave warrior." He won major, historic victories for his people and became a hero and role model. God knows our potential and the future He desires for us. God calls you brave even when you feel like a coward because he sees the brave warrior within you!

Gideon and many others in Scripture were not shining examples of valor when God first called them. In his book, *Next Door Savior*, author Max Lucado said it well when he wrote, "Contrary to what you might have been told, Jesus doesn't limit his recruitment to the stouthearted. The beat up and the worn out are prime prospects in his book, and he has been known to climb into boats, bars, and brothels, to tell them, 'It's not too late to start over and be the person I created you to be.'"

Sometimes bravery looks like taking a step even when you're feeling afraid. Other times it may look like doing nothing. Refraining from acting in your own strength to fix a situation can sometimes be scarier than taking action! But trust in God's word that says He will fight for you (Exodus 14:14).

Like Gideon, God created and called you to be brave! Hear and obey His call to courage. Then you can go from being afraid to standing up for what is right. Be still and hear God's voice speaking. He will guide your steps and remind you of the truth of who you are.

Be the brave hero God has created you to be!

MEDITATION/JOURNAL

How would you think and act if you really believed you were a brave hero? Journal your thoughts.

_____

_____

_____

_____

_____

_____

_____

_____

_____

_____

_____

_____

_____

_____

_____

_____

THE CHALLENGE

Today do something brave and valiant even if you feel afraid.

THE PRAYER

Father, I choose to act and be brave even when I feel afraid. Help me answer your call to be brave and courageous. Help me become a hero and role model for others.

THE TRANSFORMATION

How has God transformed an area of your life through today's lesson?

IN CHRIST,

I AM BRILLIANT
I AM BOLD

I AM BRAVE

I AM BLESSED
I AM BELOVED

I AM
A SON OF A GOOD FATHER

AND AN
HEIR OF A GREAT KING

DAY 17

I AM BRAVE

But Jesus turned around, and when He saw her He said, "Be of good cheer, daughter; your faith has made you well." And the woman was made well from that hour.
Matthew 9:22 (NKJV)

Courage is a choice, not a feeling. Every day, you have an inner choice to "take courage. We learned yesterday that God created you and calls you to be brave. The verse above implies that when we are unwell, either from physical sickness or from psychological and emotional wounds, we have an inner reserve of faith in Christ's power for healing. The woman in today's verse drew near to Jesus, so close that she was able to touch Him and draw upon His power by faith. At Jesus' instruction, she took courage, and by faith, she was made well. Sometimes you just have to reach out and "take courage." You have to choose to believe by faith that you will be made well. Jesus said, "If you believe, you will receive whatever you ask for in prayer" (Matthew 21:22). Wow! What a promise.

Many wonder why so many do not receive what they have asked for in prayer. The Bible gives some possible conditions to answered prayer.

1. Have faith. Don't doubt (James 1:6).
2. Ask with right motives and according to God's will (James 4:3).
3. Forgive everyone, including yourself. Bitterness, anger, jealousy, revenge, or hatred toward others may block you from total submission to God (Philippians 4:31, Matthew 6:15).
4. Pray with thanksgiving (Colossians 4:2).
5. Pray with persistence until you receive an answer (1 Thessolonians 5:16-17).

Sometimes prayers are answered in an instant, but sometimes it takes weeks, months or even years. There is an example in Scripture where a man named Daniel asked God for something, and God answered, but there was a battle in the heavens between angels and demons that lasted for over 20 days that delayed him receiving his answer from God. When you bravely believe in faith, without doubt, with love and forgiveness in your heart for all, asking with right motives, with thanksgiving and with persistence, God will answer according to his plan for you. Be Brave. Believe. Be made well.

MEDITATION/JOURNAL

Ask God to show you anything that may be blocking you from being made well. Whatever He reveals, be willing to obey. Journal your thoughts.

_____

_____

_____

_____

_____

_____

_____

_____

_____

_____

_____

_____

_____

_____

THE CHALLENGE

Draw near to Jesus. Take courage. Touch Him. Believe to be made well.

_____

THE PRAYER

Holy Spirit, help me to draw near to touch Jesus with courage and faith to be made well. Help me to ask with thanksgiving, without doubt, with right motives, with forgiving love for all, and to not give up until I have received God's answer.

_____

THE TRANSFORMATION

How has God transformed an area of your life through today's lesson?

IN CHRIST,

I AM BRILLIANT
I AM BOLD

I AM BRAVE

I AM BLESSED
I AM BELOVED

I AM
A SON OF A GOOD FATHER

AND AN
HEIR OF A GREAT KING

DAY 18

I AM BRAVE

Be on your guard; stand firm in the faith; be courageous; be strong.
1 Corinthians 16:13 (NIV)

It takes courage to go against the flow and live pure in a perverse world. It takes courage to be a true follower of Christ. You need to be brave to stand strong in your faith, even when others oppose you. You must be brave and declare, "It does not matter what my friends are doing. I choose to do what God would want me to do. Even if everyone around me is lying, I choose to tell the truth." You need to be brave, to stand up and proclaim, "I believe in God and His Word." It takes great courage to live out His Word and His ways every day.

Dr. Charles Stanley says, "Obey God, and leave all the consequences to Him." In order to do this, you have to be brave and choose to have faith in Him. The Bible says, "And without faith, it is impossible to please Him, for he who comes to God must believe that He exists and that He is a rewarder of those who seek Him." God will not disappoint those who believe. God will reward you if you will be brave and trust in Him. Your reward may not be how you envision it, and it may not be evident until Heaven, but if you courageously persevere in faith, you will be glad you did.

We will discuss tomorrow how even in a troubled world we can have peace if we courageously follow Him. There is a saying, "No Christ, No Peace, but Know Christ, Know Peace." When He is in you and you are in Him, you have peace. When you are walking in oneness with Christ's Spirit, you will walk in obedience and peace. As an old hymn put it, "Trust and obey, for there's no other way to be happy in Jesus but to trust and obey."

It is time to say "no" to your fear. It is time to say "yes" to standing firm in your faith. True Christianity is not for the faint of heart. Be brave and stand strong in your faith. God created you in his own image. He created you to be brave like Him.

MEDITATION/JOURNAL

Ask the Holy Spirit to reveal and remove any false beliefs that keep you in fear and prevent you from having a strong faith. Journal your thoughts.

_____

_____

_____

_____

_____

_____

_____

_____

_____

_____

_____

_____

_____

_____

_____

THE CHALLENGE

Decide, starting today, to be brave and to stand strong in your faith.

THE PRAYER

Father, I praise you and thank you for making me brave. Help me to courageously stand firm with a strong faith for Your glory.

THE TRANSFORMATION

How has God transformed an area of your life through today's lesson?

IN CHRIST,

I AM BRILLIANT
I AM BOLD

I AM BRAVE

I AM BLESSED
I AM BELOVED

I AM
A SON OF A GOOD FATHER

AND AN
HEIR OF A GREAT KING

DAY 19

I AM BRAVE

I have said these things, that in me you may have peace. In the world you will have tribulation and trouble. But take courage and be brave; I have overcome the world.
John 16:33

It is easy to be a Christian when all is going well. It can be difficult when you are hard pressed. Jesus did not ever promise an easy life for Christians. In fact, He said that, in this world, we would have tribulation and trouble. However, we can have courage, because He has overcome the world. The good news is God promised if we diligently seek and stick with Him through the trials of this life, He will reward us.

Be brave, and trust God in difficult or dangerous situations. Jesus said that in order to be a true follower, we must be willing to die for him. Over the past two thousand years, many Christians around the globe have paid the ultimate price for being a believer by being martyred for their faith. Just one example is the highly publicized beheadings by ISIS of Christians in the Middle East who refused to recant their faith.

What if you were given a choice between denying your faith or dying for it? The truth is, you probably will never be called upon to physically die for Christ, but you are called to die to yourself and courageously live daily for him. Will you live for him, even if you are harassed, made fun of, threatened, and slandered? Will you live for him by being honest, excellent, kind, patient, pure, forgiving, prayerful and joyful, even when it is hard?

Christ taught us that in His Kingdom, the last becomes first and the first last, the servant becomes the ruler, the one who surrenders all gains all, and the one who dies to self gains eternal life. What will you choose?

MEDITATION/JOURNAL

Think about today's Bible verse, and ask the Holy Spirit to reveal the deep, eternal truth it teaches. Journal your thoughts.

_____

_____

_____

_____

_____

_____

_____

_____

_____

_____

_____

_____

_____

_____

THE CHALLENGE

Decide to bravely be "all in," by dying to yourself and living for God, regardless of the circumstances facing you.

THE PRAYER

Holy Spirit, help me to take courage and remember that no matter what trouble I encounter in the world, Jesus has overcome the world!

THE TRANSFORMATION

How has God transformed an area of your life through today's lesson?

IN CHRIST,

I AM BRILLIANT
I AM BOLD

I AM BRAVE

I AM BLESSED
I AM BELOVED

I AM
A SON OF A GOOD FATHER

AND AN
HEIR OF A GREAT KING

DAY 20

I AM BRAVE

To the one who is victorious and does my will to the end, I will give authority over the nations—
Revelation 2:26 (NIV)

As we discussed yesterday, we all need to take courage because even though in this world you will have trouble, Jesus has overcome the world! The good news is that if Jesus lives in you and you are surrendered to His indwelling power, you are an overcomer, too! The paramount priority is to never give up. The Scripture says we will get the prize if we finish the race (Philippians 3:13-14). We will reap a reward if we do not give up.

Endure. Stay with it. Keep moving forward even when you feel like throwing in the towel. Being a Christian is not an easy life, but it is a blessed life if you are all in. Do not be lukewarm or a half-in/half-out Christian. Those Christians are usually miserable. You do not have to be perfect. "All in" Christians still stumble, but when they mess up, by God's grace, they get back up and keep moving forward.

You will be so glad you continued to courageously overcome when you meet Jesus face-to-face and He says to you, "Well done, good and faithful servant. Come receive your reward." We are not saved from punishment by our good works but by "grace through faith." However, we are promised to be rewarded for what we do for Christ in love.

You have it in you to be "more than a conqueror" in Christ Jesus. So be all in until the end, and in the end you will be so glad you were brave and did it!

MEDITATION/JOURNAL

Think about today's Bible verse. Imagine yourself finishing well at the end of your life and being rewarded face-to-face with Jesus. Journal your thoughts.

THE CHALLENGE

All day today, do your best to obey Him from beginning until the end!

_____

THE PRAYER

Father, help me to courageously overcome and to obey to the end so that I may finish well.

_____

THE TRANSFORMATION

How has God transformed an area of your life through today's lesson?

IN CHRIST,

I AM BRILLIANT
I AM BOLD

I AM BRAVE

I AM BLESSED
I AM BELOVED

I AM
A SON OF A GOOD FATHER

AND AN
HEIR OF A GREAT KING

DAY 21

I AM BRAVE

Finally, be strong and brave in the Lord and in the strength of His might. Put on the full armor of God, so that you will be able to stand firm against the schemes of the devil.
Ephesians 6:10-11 (NIV)

Strength and bravery are part of your inheritance in Christ. Be brave and be strong, not in your own strength, but in the supernatural strength of the King's might. It's part of your spiritual armor.

What does the Bible say about the full armor of God? "Stand, therefore, with truth like a belt around your waist, righteousness like armor on your chest, and your feet sandaled with readiness for the gospel of peace. In every situation take the shield of faith, and with it you will be able to extinguish all the flaming arrows of the evil one. Take the helmet of salvation, and the sword of the Spirit, which is God's word. Pray at all times in the Spirit with every prayer and request, and stay alert in this with all perseverance and intercession for all the saints" (Ephesians 6:11-18).

The breastplate of righteousness holds up all the other pieces of our armor, because Christ's righteousness is our breastplate against the arrows and attacks of the enemy. Our feet should be shod with the preparation of the gospel of peace. The shield of faith quenches the darts of temptation. Salvation must be our helmet. Notice there is no armor piece to cover a Christian's back, because a Christian is never to turn back in battle.

There is only one weapon of defense, and that is the sword of the Spirit, which is the Word of God. Jesus fought Satan with the Word of God and won his battle in the desert. A single verse, if rightly applied, helps us say "no" to temptation and defeats our enemy. Perseverence in prayer is the binding which keeps together all other parts of the armor.

Spiritual strength and bravery are needed for spiritual warfare. Put on, and do not take off, your armor until your warfare is finished. Your combat is not against human enemies, but against a supernatural enemy. We do have a real enemy, whose goal is to wound, conquer, and even kill us in battle. He hopes to catch us without our armor on.

If you will daily put on your spiritual armor, you will find yourself equipped to not only stand strong against the devil's schemes, but also to take ground and to be more than a conqueror in battle.

MEDITATION/JOURNAL

Imagine yourself putting on each piece of the armor of God. Journal your thoughts.

_____

_____

_____

_____

_____

_____

_____

_____

_____

_____

_____

_____

_____

_____

_____

THE CHALLENGE

In prayer today, put on the full armor of God listed in scripture and in this devotional.

_____

THE PRAYER

Father, I choose to prepare myself daily to be strong and brave in the strength of the Almighty by putting on the full armor of God. Help me to be fully equipped to stand firm against the enemy's schemes and to be victorious in every battle.

_____

THE TRANSFORMATION

How has God transformed an area of your life through today's lesson?

Week 4

I AM
BLESSED

IN CHRIST,

I AM BRILLIANT
I AM BOLD
I AM BRAVE

I AM BLESSED

I AM BELOVED

I AM
A SON OF A GOOD FATHER

AND AN
HEIR OF A GREAT KING

DAY 22

I AM BLESSED

The Lord bless you and keep you. The Lord make His face shine on you and be gracious to you. The Lord lift up His countenance on you, and give you peace.
Numbers 6:24-26 (NIV)

You are blessed! This statement and this verse may bring up questions in your mind. What does it mean to be "blessed" by the Lord? Why is this a good thing? How can I be blessed by the Lord?

What is this sacred blessing from Scripture all about? Long ago, God instructed His people to have their priest speak this blessing over them daily as a benediction. When His people had this blessing pronounced over them, God promised not only to bless them Himself but to give His peace to them. The Hebrew word for "blessing" means literally to kneel down bestowing a gift, a mercy, or a grace that brings great benefit. The original meaning of the blessing above is, "The Lord will kneel before you presenting gifts and will guard you with a hedge of protection. The Lord will illuminate the wholeness of his being toward you, bringing order and beautifying you. The Lord will lift up his wholeness of being to look upon you; he will set in place all you need to be whole."

God promises to give us His peace. The Hebrew word for "peace" is shalom. If you receive the fullness of His gift of shalom, you not only have peace but prosperity, protection, power, and complete wholeness, with nothing broken or missing.

A benediction means literally "good spoken." Notice that the Lord's name is spoken three times in this blessing. This mystery is revealed to be God in three persons: Father, Son and Holy Spirit. Life and death, as well as blessings and curses, lie in the power of the spoken word. In fact, God created worlds with His Words. Because of Jesus, we no longer need a priest to bless us, because we are now pronounced as priests. There is great power in speaking words of blessing over yourself and others when spoken in faith.

How can you be "blessed"? You can be blessed by believing and receiving the gift of God's Grace for you, by speaking words of blessing over your own and others' lives, and through obedience to His Word.

MEDITATION/JOURNAL

Visualize the Father kneeling down and blessing you. Journal your thoughts.

_____

_____

_____

_____

_____

_____

_____

_____

_____

_____

_____

_____

_____

_____

_____

THE CHALLENGE

Memorize today's Scripture. Speak these verses over yourself every day. For example, "The Lord my Father is blessing me, protecting me, making His face shine upon me and giving me His Shalom Peace."

THE PRAYER

Father, I choose to speak, believe and receive the gift of your blessing on my life. Thank you for the gifts of your peace, your love and your wholeness in my life.

THE TRANSFORMATION

How has God transformed an area of your life through today's lesson?

IN CHRIST,

I AM BRILLIANT
I AM BOLD
I AM BRAVE

I AM BLESSED

I AM BELOVED

I AM
A SON OF A GOOD FATHER

AND AN
HEIR OF A GREAT KING

DAY 23

I AM BLESSED

But blessed is the one who trusts in the Lord, whose confidence is in Him. They will be like a tree planted by the water that sends out its roots by the stream. It does not fear when heat comes; its leaves are always green. It has no worries in a year of drought and never fails to bear fruit.
Jeremiah 17:7-8 (NIV)

Jesus remained rooted in His Father. He often retreated alone to a quiet place to pray (Luke 5:16). He did not rely on His own strength to face the crowds or the difficulties He would encounter throughout His ministry and mission. He knew the importance of praying and being in the presence of His Father. He needed that intimacy to keep moving forward. He only did what His Father told Him to do, and that required continually meeting with and hearing from God (John 8:28).

Likewise, it is your dependence on God that enables you to confidently encounter daily situations and challenges. Imagine the power you would receive from your Father, the Creator of the universe, if you met with Him an hour each day before you faced the world! When we seek Him, He blesses us with a fresh filling of His Holy Spirit who was sent to guide us so we don't have to lean on our own understanding. As we lean on the guidance of the Holy Spirit each day, we are practicing trusting Him. The more we practice this, the more our faith and trust will grow. We will be blessed when our confidence and trust is in Him!

When we follow Him, He keeps us on the right path, because He knows all things. He gives us the wisdom we need to make right choices, and He shows us the way of blessing. How can we be the tree that is always green, that never fears and never fails to bear fruit? By keeping our roots planted by the water. What does that mean? You plant yourself in Christ when you stay in His Word and flow with His Spirit. Jesus said something similar, "If you abide in me and I in you, then you will never fail to bear fruit" (John 15:7).

By planting ourselves in Christ, staying in His Word, and drinking from His Spirit, we can remain rooted in Him and anchored into the stream of Living Water. Even in dry times, His Word and Spirit do not run dry. Stay rooted in the streams of His Spirit so you don't either.

MEDITATION/JOURNAL

Think about a situation where you have felt overwhelmed recently, and imagine how it would feel if you let go and let God take control of the details. Picture yourself full of the Holy Spirit as you walk out this situation. Journal your thoughts.

_____

_____

_____

_____

_____

_____

_____

_____

_____

_____

_____

_____

_____

_____

THE CHALLENGE

Make a commitment to read the Bible every day.

THE PRAYER

Father, I want to be blessed and continually bear good fruit. Help me to stay planted in You and Your Word and to send out my roots into the flowing stream of your Spirit.

THE TRANSFORMATION

How has God transformed an area of your life through today's lesson?

IN CHRIST,

I AM BRILLIANT
I AM BOLD
I AM BRAVE

I AM BLESSED

I AM BELOVED

I AM
A SON OF A GOOD FATHER

AND AN
HEIR OF A GREAT KING

DAY 24

I AM BLESSED

For if you are insulted or ridiculed because of the name of Christ, you are blessed,
for the Spirit of glory and of God rests on you.
1 Peter 4:14 (NIV)

If you find yourself being made fun of or insulted because you are a Christian, count yourself blessed! There is a glory that rests upon you and your life if people are noticing that you are a true follower of Christ.

The ways of God are not the ways of man. When others witness Christ's ways in action through you, they may at first think you are weird—until you win them over with your kindness. The Bible says that we are to overcome evil, not with evil, but with good. In doing so, you can bring conviction to those around you.

Jesus took this a step further when He said, "Love your enemies and bless those who curse you, do good to those who hate you, and pray for those who spitefully use you and persecute you" (Matthew 5:44, NKJV). His instructions also say to pray and do good things for those who mistreat you. There is power in blessing that is far greater than the power of cursing. God's Word instructs us, "If your enemy is hungry, feed him; if he is thirsty, give him a drink; For in so doing you will heap coals of fire on his head"(Romans 12:20, NKJV).

Civil Rights leader and minister, Dr. Martin Luther King, Jr., said, "Hate does not drive out hate, only love can do that." Similarly, darkness does not drive out darkness; only light can do that. Be the light that drives out the darkness. Be the love that drives out hate. Be the blessing that conquers the curse.

MEDITATION/JOURNAL

Meditate on seeing your enemies transformed by your prayers, blessing, and kindness. Journal your thoughts.

_____

_____

_____

_____

_____

_____

_____

_____

_____

_____

_____

_____

_____

THE CHALLENGE

When someone mistreats or literally curses you this week, choose to be kind to them and bless them. Pray for them and seek to be a blessing to them.

THE PRAYER

Holy Spirit, help me to bless others regardless of how they treat me. Help me to bless those that curse me. Help me to be good to those who treat me badly.

THE TRANSFORMATION

How has God transformed an area of your life through today's lesson?

IN CHRIST,

I AM BRILLIANT
I AM BOLD
I AM BRAVE

I AM BLESSED

I AM BELOVED

I AM
A SON OF A GOOD FATHER

AND AN
HEIR OF A GREAT KING

DAY 25

I AM BLESSED

And I will make you a great nation, and I will bless you, and make your name great;
and so you shall be a blessing.
Genesis 12:2

This promise from Scripture was given to Abraham and his descendants. The Bible teaches that by faith through God's grace we can inherit the promises in Scripture. A principle in God's Word is that we are blessed to be a blessing. The Bible also teaches that we are ambassadors of Christ and His love. We are to seek to make God's name famous by how we represent Him in the world. When we are blessed, we demonstrate the goodness of the God of blessing. As we learned earlier, blessing is not necessarily wealth or power but rather love, joy and peace. The truly blessed one is the one who holds a certain hope and expectation of blessing.

God blesses us, not just so we in ourselves can experience blessing, but so we can go out and bless others. In the world, when we receive a blessing such as a piece of candy, and we give it away, that piece is gone. However, in God's Kingdom, when we give something away, like our love, it multiplies. Likewise, when we share a thought with another person or group, that idea multiplies.

Jesus demonstrated this principle by taking five loaves of bread and two fish offered to him by a little boy. After praying and blessing them, he went on to feed over 5,000 people. Through prayer, thanksgiving, and the dunamis power of God, this meager offering was multiplied so there were even twelve large baskets of leftovers.

Jesus said that whoever believes in Him would do the things He did and even greater (John 14:12)! Without faith, it is impossible, but if we believe without doubting, we can be blessed to do all things through Christ who gives us strength (Philippians 4:13). God's math is not the same as our math. He is the God of impossibilities: multiplying fish and loaves, providing manna from heaven, and performing miracles unfathomable. Even today, there are documented examples of missionaries in Mozambique, Africa, seeing food multiplied. With God's blessing, all things are possible. When you bless others, you are blessed.

MEDITATION/JOURNAL

See yourself in faith performing miracles. Journal your thoughts.

_____

_____

_____

_____

_____

_____

_____

_____

_____

_____

_____

_____

_____

_____

_____

THE CHALLENGE

Decide to be a blessing to others today.

THE PRAYER

Father, bless me that I might be a blessing. Help me spread and expand your Kingdom and multiply its blessing by sharing Jesus with others.

THE TRANSFORMATION

How has God transformed an area of your life through today's lesson?

IN CHRIST,

I AM BRILLIANT
I AM BOLD
I AM BRAVE

I AM BLESSED

I AM BELOVED

I AM
A SON OF A GOOD FATHER

AND AN
HEIR OF A GREAT KING

DAY 26

I AM BLESSED

Whoever gives heed to the Lord's Word and instruction finds good and prospers;
blessed is the one who trusts in the Lord.
Proverbs 16:20 (NIV)

We answered the question yesterday of how you can be blessed. The simple answer is we are blessed by believing and receiving the gift of God's grace for us, speaking words of blessing over our own and others' lives, and through obedience to His Word. Today's verse again reminds us that we receive blessing when we obey and heed God's Word and instruction. When we read and hide God's Word in our heart, then diligently seek to apply it to our lives, good will come to us.

Obeying God's Word and trusting God go hand in hand. The blessed person puts his trust in the Lord, not in himself, others or worldly wealth. The blessed person is not just a hearer of the Word but a diligent doer of the Word. When you seek to find God's will for your life, you also find God's good for your life. Blessing comes when we trust God in our present and for our future. When we seek God's Kingdom and righteousness first, we will receive all kinds of good things in return. The Scripture even says that those who sacrifice houses, land or seeing their family will be given back those very things in this life and in the life to come.

When you trust God for everything and in everything, you cannot go wrong. The good news is that God has promised to reward us if we diligently seek and stick with Him.

MEDITATION/JOURNAL

Think about today's Bible verse, and ask the Holy Spirit to reveal the deep, eternal truth it teaches.

THE CHALLENGE

Decide to trust God and obey His Word and instructions.

THE PRAYER

Holy Spirit, help me to trust completely and to heed your voice of instruction through prayer and through Your Word.

THE TRANSFORMATION

How has God transformed an area of your life through today's lesson?

IN CHRIST,

I AM BRILLIANT
I AM BOLD
I AM BRAVE

I AM BLESSED

I AM BELOVED

I AM
A SON OF A GOOD FATHER

AND AN
HEIR OF A GREAT KING

DAY 27

I AM BLESSED

Blessed are the poor in spirit, for theirs is the kingdom of heaven. Blessed are those who mourn, for they will be comforted. Blessed are the meek, for they will inherit the earth. Blessed are those who hunger and thirst after righteousness, for they will be filled. Blessed are the merciful, for they shall be shown mercy. Blessed are the pure in heart, for they will see God. Blessed are the peacemakers, for they will be called the sons of God. Blessed are those who are persecuted because of righteousness, for theirs is the kingdom of heaven. Blessed are you when people insult you, persecute you and falsely say all kinds of evil against you because of me. Rejoice and be glad, because great is your reward in heaven, for in the same way they persecuted the prophets who were before you.
Matthew 5:3-12 (NIV)

The above verses come from Jesus' famous Sermon on the Mount. Jesus' radical words in this sermon truly turned the world on its head. He explained the way to prosper in His kingdom is to humbly serve all. We are blessed when we live a counter-culture life and take the lowest place. The last shall become first; the servant of all becomes the ruler of all.

Scripture tells us there will be troubles and suffering of many kinds in this world, even to the point of persecution. But, we must look past what we experience and seek His supernatural provision in every situation. This is why it is important to count the cost of being a Christian and become poor in spirit. We must empty ourselves by laying our preferences and grievances before the Lord so we will hunger for and be filled with HIS Spirit.

Romans 5:3 says to rejoice in our suffering, which produces endurance, character, and hope, and that does not put us to shame because God's love has been poured into our hearts through the Holy Spirit. God promises to bless and comfort us if we persevere and courageously continue to follow Jesus. "Those who sow in tears will reap with songs of joy" (Psalm 126:5). He will dry our tears and turn our sorrow into joy.

MEDITATION/JOURNAL

Imagine yourself being truly blessed as you follow Jesus. Journal your thoughts.

_____

_____

_____

_____

_____

_____

_____

_____

_____

_____

_____

_____

_____

_____

THE CHALLENGE

Think about today's Bible verse. Imagine yourself being blessed by living a counter-culture life in the opposite spirit of this world's system.

_____

THE PRAYER

Father, help me to courageously overcome and to obey Jesus' principles, and help me to be humble in everything so that I might be truly blessed.

_____

THE TRANSFORMATION

How has God transformed an area of your life through today's lesson?

IN CHRIST,

I AM BRILLIANT
I AM BOLD
I AM BRAVE

I AM BLESSED

I AM BELOVED

I AM
A SON OF A GOOD FATHER

AND AN
HEIR OF A GREAT KING

DAY 28

I AM BLESSED

And all these blessings shall come upon you and overtake you, because you obey the voice of the Lord your God: You will be blessed everywhere you go and in everything you do; your work will be blessed; your children will be blessed; God will cause the defeat of your enemies; God will command the blessing on you and your storehouses and all you put your hand to; God will bless you in the land He gives you; God will open the windows of Heaven such that you do not have room to hold it all; You will lend to many but borrow from none; God will make you the head and not the tail, above only and not beneath so long as you diligently obey the voice of the Lord.
Paraphrase of Deuteronomy 28

How would it feel to have blessings chase you down? How can you experience that? In Deuteronomy 28, God clearly tells the Isrealites how to receive His blessings through obedience. He promises blessings to rain upon us as His children when we seek His will and follow His voice. It is vital to learn to hear His voice, as it leads to untold treasures!

The primary way He speaks to us is through the Bible, the inspired written Word of God. This is the guidebook for our lives. God also speaks to us through His Holy Spirit, our counselor and comforter, who lives inside us and guides us into all truth (John 14:26). He speaks to us in dreams, visions, art, song, and through other people and circumstances. God communicates to us in times of prayer, in moments of quiet, and in feelings of peace. The Book of 1 Kings 19:12 says God speaks to us in a still, small voice.

However you hear Him, God's voice brings conviction but never condemnation; peace and not anxiety; order and not confusion. His voice will never contradict His Word in the scriptures. If what you hear involves taking controversial action, always submit it to two or more trusted and wise Christian friends for counsel.

We can sometimes go on autopilot, wrongly assuming we know all the answers, relying on our own understanding rather than leaning on the Holy Spirit. Instead, we should take time to inquire of the Lord (Psalm 34:4). There is no better counsel than from the supremely wise Holy Spirit.

As you seek His will, discern His voice and diligently obey, you will be blessed!

MEDITATION/JOURNAL

Ask your Heavenly Father to speak to you through His Spirit and His Word. Write down what you hear. Always test what you hear with two trusted, wise Christian friends/counselors.

_____

_____

_____

_____

_____

_____

_____

_____

_____

_____

_____

_____

_____

THE CHALLENGE

Seek to hear God's voice today in a way you have not before. For example, open the Bible and ask God to speak to you through His Word. Write down what you believe He is telling you.

THE PRAYER

Father, I choose to daily seek to grow in hearing your voice and diligently obeying what you say. I believe blessing will chase me down and overtake me as I seek to follow your voice. Bless me, Father, so that I may be a blessing to others.

THE TRANSFORMATION

How has God transformed an area of your life through today's lesson?

Week 5

I AM
BELOVED

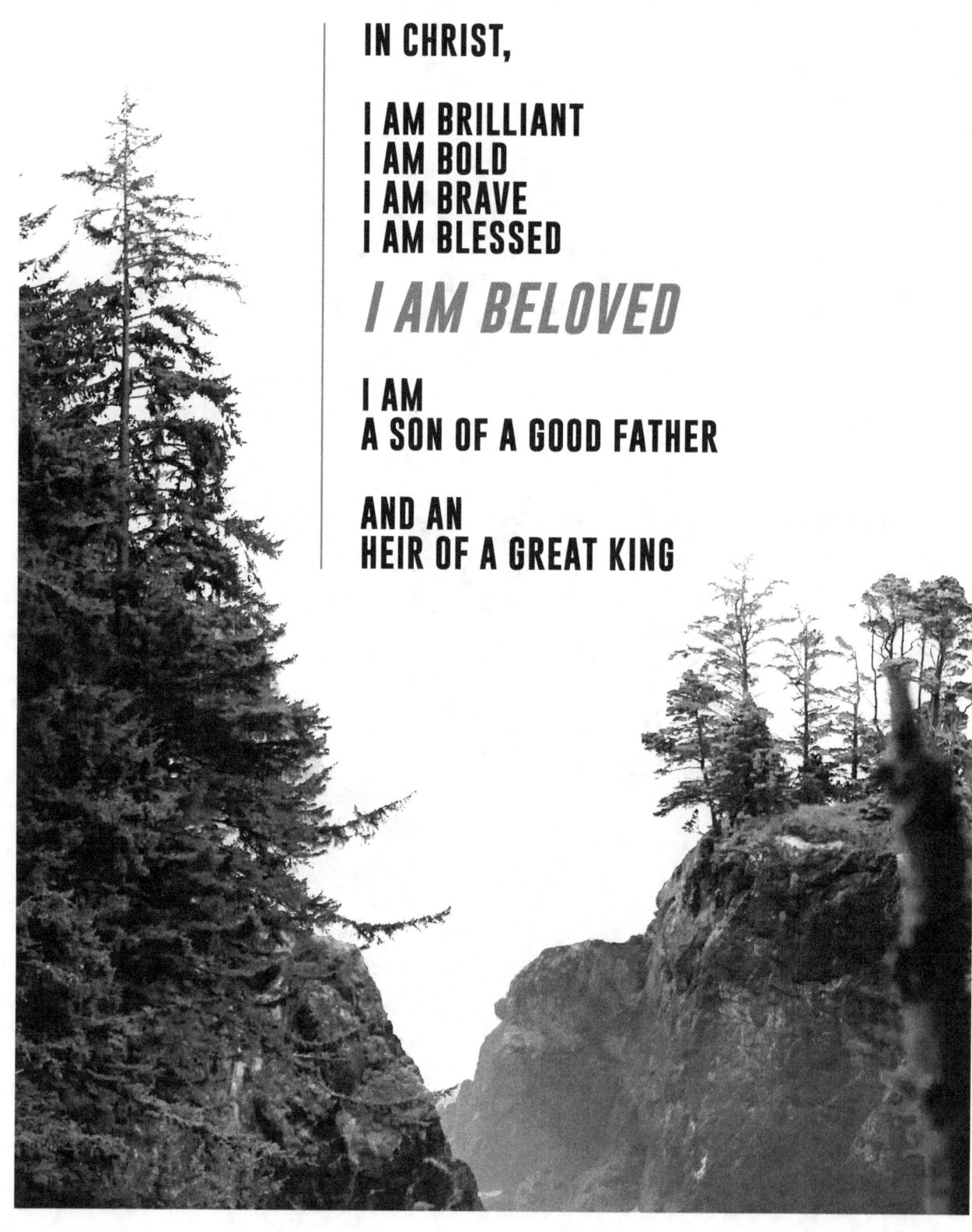

IN CHRIST,

I AM BRILLIANT
I AM BOLD
I AM BRAVE
I AM BLESSED

I AM BELOVED

I AM
A SON OF A GOOD FATHER

AND AN
HEIR OF A GREAT KING

DAY 29

I AM BELOVED

I am my beloved's and my beloved is mine.
Song of Songs 6:3 (NIV)

You are beloved! This statement and this Bible verse may bring up questions in your mind, like, "What does it mean to be beloved of the Lord?" It means that you are wanted. Its means you belong and are part of a family. It means that you are adored.

The book of Songs of Songs—also known as Song of Solomon—is a love song that was probably written by King Solomon. There are different views of how this book of the Bible is to be understood. The consensus is that it describes both a romantic love between a bride and bridegroom, and at the same time, God's love for His people.

Christians are considered children of the Father, but we are also called the "Bride of Christ" because of the passionate love Jesus has for us. It may sound funny for men to be called a "bride," but it's just the way God refers to His relationship with the church—like a romance between a bride and bridegroom. Song of Songs reveals God's pattern of how we grow in passion for Christ. The "beloved" in the story represents the Bride of Christ, who begins loving her bridegroom with an immature love. Throughout the book, her love—like ours—becomes more mature, until it reaches full maturity. This provides us a picture of how our love for Jesus can also reach maturity.

If you are your beloved's, that means that you belong to Him. It means you are committed for life to Him—not only out of obligation but also out of desire. He has won your heart. He has captivated your affection. He wants to be there for you, to comfort, counsel, console and captivate you.

May you fall in love forever with Jesus. He is crazy about you! May you belong to Him, and He to you, for eternity.

MEDITATION/JOURNAL

Think of yourself as the Bride of Christ and about Jesus as your Bridegroom, and feel His affection for you. Journal your thoughts.

_____

_____

_____

_____

_____

_____

_____

_____

_____

_____

_____

_____

_____

THE CHALLENGE

Memorize today's scripture. Speak it over yourself every day.

THE PRAYER

Jesus, help me to fall in love with you and to feel your deep affection toward me. Captivate and capture my heart. I want to belong to you. Be my beloved.

THE TRANSFORMATION

How has God transformed an area of your life through today's lesson?

IN CHRIST,

I AM BRILLIANT
I AM BOLD
I AM BRAVE
I AM BLESSED

I AM BELOVED

I AM
A SON OF A GOOD FATHER

AND AN
HEIR OF A GREAT KING

DAY 30

I AM BELOVED

In this the love of God was made manifest among us, that God sent his only Son into the world, so that
we might live through him. In this is love, not that we have loved
God but that he loved us and sent his Son to be the propitiation for our sins.
Beloved, if God so loved us, we also ought to love one another.
1 John 4:9-11 (NKJV)

God calls you his beloved. He loves you, not because you loved him, but because God is love. He died for you that you might live through Him and become His child. Ephesians 1:5 says He died for you that you might become the adopted child of God.

There is a saying that hurting people hurt people. Similarly, loved people love people. When you experience and receive the deep, wonderful, rich, transforming love of God, you are able to love others with that same love you have received. You cannot give away something you do not have. In other words, you are able to love others only with the love you have received.

The Spirit of the Lord – the Spirit of love – lives inside those who truly follow Christ. If someone does not love the image of the Creator in his people, they do not truly love God. God has shown himself to be love through his actions. Has there ever been a more glorious display of love than Christ dying on the cross for those who cannot earn or deserve this sacrifice? His sacrifice was an unfathomable cost, but His gift is freely given so you might freely give His love to others.

A Christian who has experienced the depth and value of the extravagant love of Christ is transformed by that love. As a result, our heart's desire is to pour out this love upon others.

MEDITATION/JOURNAL

Imagine Jesus paying the price for your sins on the cross. How does it feel to know how much He loves you? Journal your thoughts.

_____

_____

_____

_____

_____

_____

_____

_____

_____

_____

_____

_____

_____

THE CHALLENGE

Show your love today to someone who wronged you and therefore may feel undeserving of your love. Allow them to experience God's unconditional love and mercy, just as you have.

THE PRAYER

Father, help me to receive your free gift of love that I might be able to freely give your love to others.

THE TRANSFORMATION

How has God transformed an area of your life through today's lesson?

IN CHRIST,

I AM BRILLIANT
I AM BOLD
I AM BRAVE
I AM BLESSED

I AM BELOVED

I AM
A SON OF A GOOD FATHER

AND AN
HEIR OF A GREAT KING

DAY 31

I AM BELOVED

God, being rich in mercy, because of the great love with which he loved us, even when we were dead in our trespasses, made us alive together with Christ - by grace you have been saved.
Ephesians 2:4-5 (NKJV)

Have you ever known someone who was so kind that loving them felt easy? On the other hand, have you ever known anyone who was mean or unkind, and you found it hard to love them (or even like them)?

The scripture above tells us that while we were dead in our trespasses (sins or mistakes), God loved us. What does being dead in our trespasses mean? Before we received Jesus and forgiveness for our sins, we were dead in spirit. When we receive Christ's forgiveness, we become alive in spirit.

God doesn't look upon us and decide to love us because we've done something good or because we are kind or lovable. He offers His grace to us because of His great mercy, and He loves us with a perfect and enduring love, even when we are at our very worst. We are saved by grace, and there is absolutely nothing we can do to earn our salvation, eternal life, or good standing with God. It's all because of His kindness and mercy, and He looks upon us with a Father's heart and feels compassion for us, even when we are at our very worst.

God isn't stingy with His mercy. Instead, He is rich and generous. That means no matter how bad we have been or what we have done, God's mercy is greater than our sin. So come to Him, knowing that He does not condemn you for mistakes. He offers you His rich mercy, complete forgiveness, and love.

MEDITATION/JOURNAL

Imagine receiving God's love and mercy for you. Imagine Him telling you how much He loves you, even when you feel at your very worst. Journal your thoughts.

_____

_____

_____

_____

_____

_____

_____

_____

_____

_____

_____

_____

_____

THE CHALLENGE

Focus on giving God's love to someone who needs to be shown mercy.

THE PRAYER

Father, help us to receive your rich love and give it richly to others today.

THE TRANSFORMATION

How has God transformed an area of your life through today's lesson?

IN CHRIST,

I AM BRILLIANT
I AM BOLD
I AM BRAVE
I AM BLESSED

I AM BELOVED

I AM
A SON OF A GOOD FATHER

AND AN
HEIR OF A GREAT KING

DAY 32

I AM BELOVED

Beloved, let us love one another, for love is from God, and whoever loves has been born of God and knows God. Anyone who does not love does not know God, because God is love.
1 John 4:7-8 (NKJV)

To know God is to know love. When you truly know love from the perfect source, you cannot help but love others.

When we have been treated poorly or abused by others, especially the people who were supposed to love us the most, we can sometimes find it difficult to receive God's love. If we have learned we cannot trust people, it is hard to trust God.

The truth is, people, life, and this world will let you down sometimes. But God promises that if we will trust and obey him, He will ultimately work all things (even the horrible things, even your own sinful things) together for good (Romans 8:28). Our part in seeing this accomplished is that we love Him (turn our hearts towards Him) and follow Him in the direction He leads.

How do you love God and turn your heart towards Him? Jesus said, "If you love me, you will obey my commands" (John 14:15). Jesus also said, "For where your treasure is, there will your heart be also" (Matthew 6:21). Your treasure includes your time, energy, money, and talents. Your heart will follow your thoughts, your choices, and your actions, so you have to treasure the right things by investing your thoughts, talents, time, and actions into obediently following Him.

MEDITATION/JOURNAL

What is your treasure? How do you invest your time, your money, and your talents? Journal your thoughts.

_____

_____

_____

_____

_____

_____

_____

_____

_____

_____

_____

_____

_____

THE CHALLENGE

Decide to invest your treasure in Jesus today by leading your heart to obediently follow Him.

THE PRAYER

Father, help me to wholeheartedly invest my treasure in You so that my heart is turned towards You. Help me to truly love You.

THE TRANSFORMATION

How has God transformed an area of your life through today's lesson?

IN CHRIST,

I AM BRILLIANT
I AM BOLD
I AM BRAVE
I AM BLESSED

I AM BELOVED

I AM
A SON OF A GOOD FATHER

AND AN
HEIR OF A GREAT KING

DAY 33

I AM BELOVED

I have been crucified with Christ. It is no longer I who live, but Christ who lives in me. And the life I now live in the flesh I live by faith in the Son of God who loved me and gave himself for me.
Galatians 2:20 (NKJV)

Do you love a good mystery? In Galatians, Paul writes about one of the greatest mysteries mentioned in the Bible. He says he has been crucified with Christ. What on Earth does he mean by that?

When Christ was crucified, He died. When we receive Christ as our Savior, we must die to ourselves, surrendering everything in our lives to God. In Galatians 20:12, it tells us that we escaped the penalty of sin to live a life that pleases God. Knowing that we are "crucified with Christ" is great news! We have the power to say "no" to sin and "yes" to God. If you sincerely live for God, it is not you living, but Jesus living in you, giving you His power and His love.

So, here is the mystery: how can Jesus live in you? By faith! You have to believe that Jesus lives in you as you choose to follow Him and die to yourself, or "crucify yourself." Remember, He was God's payment for our sin—yours and mine. So in essence, our sin was with Him when He was crucified. In His great love for us, He chose to pay the ultimate price through suffering and dying a terrible, painful death. Jesus didn't do it because humanity seemed particularly lovable. In fact, the Bible makes it clear that even though we were unlovable and unworthy, Jesus still decided to sacrifice His life for us. Clearly, this is an amazing love, difficult for us to comprehend—a beautiful mystery indeed. This is His love toward you, His beloved.

Christ invested His greatest treasure – His very life – for you because He loves you. May you show your love for Him and invest your treasure—your life—for Him. Die daily to yourself so He might daily live with and through you. Jesus likened the Kingdom of God to a treasure hidden in a field. A wise merchant sold everything he had to purchase the field, knowing that the hidden treasure was far greater than all he had owned before (Matthew 13:44). When we give our life to Jesus, it is like giving Him our brown paper bag lunch and receiving a great feast in exchange. Exchanging our life for His is the greatest and wisest exchange we will ever make!

MEDITATION/JOURNAL

Meditate on Christ's amazing love, and how He loved us even when we were unlovable. Journal your thoughts.

_____

_____

_____

_____

_____

_____

_____

_____

_____

_____

_____

_____

_____

_____

THE CHALLENGE

Spend five minutes thinking of areas of your life you need to surrender to God. When you surrender those areas to God, you "crucify" them, and Jesus takes up residence there instead. Imagine literally surrendering your hate or unforgiveness and receiving Christ's love in its place.

THE PRAYER

Heavenly Father, help me give you my life and receive your great life and love in return. Help me have an encounter with your love. When I realize I am loved, I can trust and surrender every area to be crucified with Christ.

THE TRANSFORMATION

How has God transformed an area of your life through today's lesson?

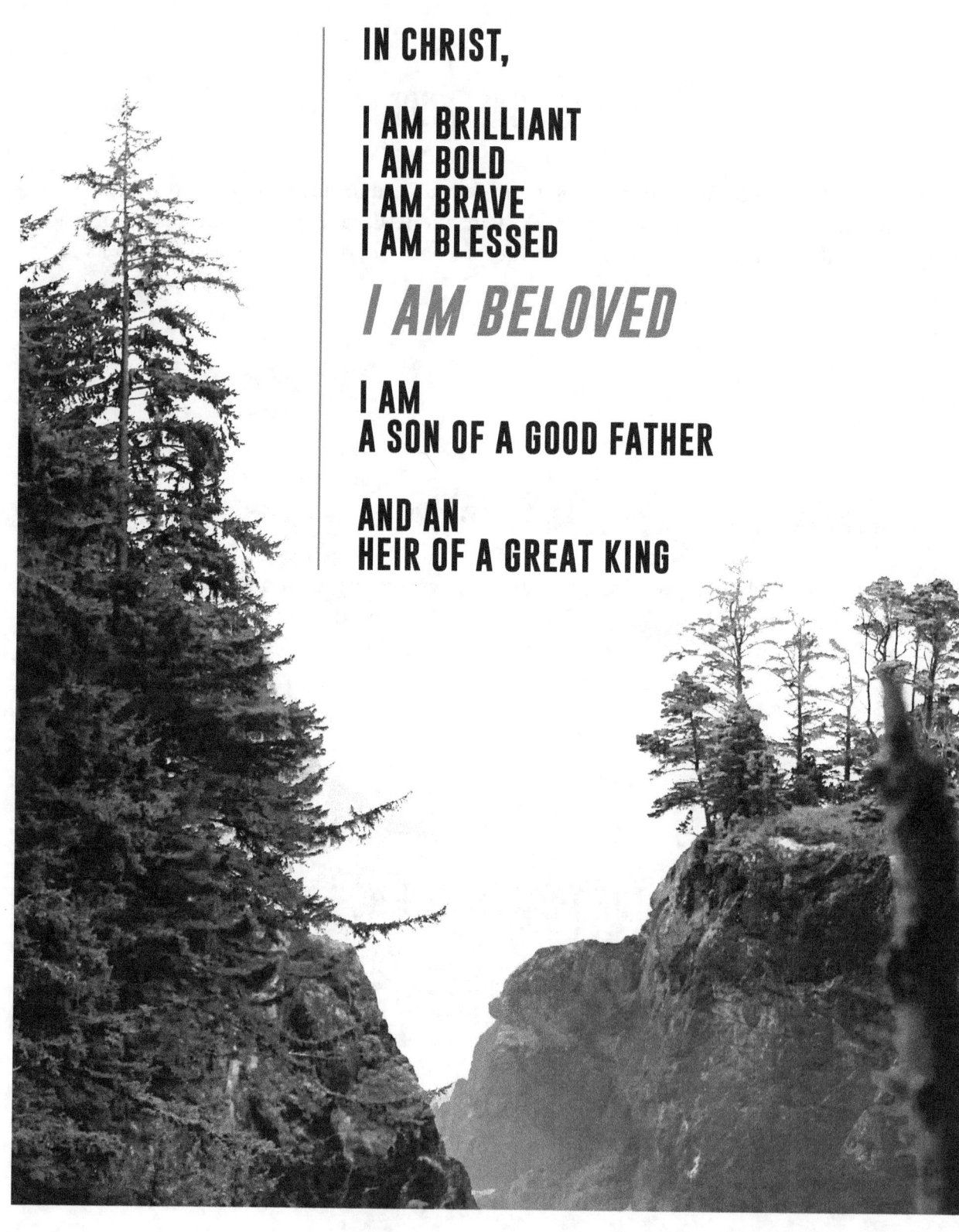

IN CHRIST,

I AM BRILLIANT
I AM BOLD
I AM BRAVE
I AM BLESSED

I AM BELOVED

I AM
A SON OF A GOOD FATHER

AND AN
HEIR OF A GREAT KING

DAY 34

I AM BELOVED

No, in all these things we are more than conquerors through Him who loved us. For I am convinced that neither death nor life, neither angels nor demons, neither the present nor the future, nor any powers, neither height nor depth, nor anything else in all creation, will be able to separate us from the love of God that is in Christ Jesus our Lord.
Romans 8:37-39 (NIV)

The Great Exchange is when you surrender your life completely to Jesus, trading your sinful nature for His righteousness. He becomes your beloved and you become His. You belong to Christ and Christ belongs to you. He promises to love you so much that literally nothing will separate you from His love.

If you have been easily conquered in the past by the deceptive lure of sin, the persuasion of others, or your own selfishness, guess what? You can start having the strength to be and do everything He has created you for by submitting to His power that is now at work within you. He is your conquering King! And under His command, you are more than a conqueror.

God is the most powerful being in the universe, and once you have made the Great Exchange, He, His power, and His love live inside you. Imagine that! Christ the King of Kings, God of Angel Armies, Warrior of Warriors lives in and through you as much as you allow Him to! No wonder Paul in the Bible, after surrendering His life to Christ, said, "I can do all things through Christ who gives me strength" (Philippians 4:13 NKJV).

MEDITATION/JOURNAL

What does it mean to you when it says in Philippians 4:13 that you can "do all things through Christ" who gives you strength? Journal your thoughts.

_____

_____

_____

_____

_____

_____

_____

_____

_____

_____

_____

_____

_____

_____

_____

THE CHALLENGE

Think about today's Bible verse. Imagine what your life might look like if you made the Great Exchange and Christ ruled as a conquering King on the throne of your life. You, through His power within you, would be a conquer also.

_____

THE PRAYER

My Father, my King, live and reign through me. I want to be more than a conqueror over sin and selfishness. Reveal Your wisdom and help me make the Great Exchange and never turn back. I want to belong to you and you to me. Let me never be separated from your love.

_____

THE TRANSFORMATION

How has God transformed an area of your life through today's lesson?

IN CHRIST,

I AM BRILLIANT
I AM BOLD
I AM BRAVE
I AM BLESSED

I AM BELOVED

I AM
A SON OF A GOOD FATHER

AND AN
HEIR OF A GREAT KING

DAY 35

I AM BELOVED

Therefore be imitators of God, as beloved children; and walk in love, just as Christ loved you
and gave Himself up for us, an offering and a sacrifice to God as a fragrant aroma.
Ephesians 5:1-2 (NKJV)

When you adore, love and admire someone, you want to be like them. Children who have a father or mother they dearly love will often grow up to be like them. Have you heard the saying, "Like father, like son?"

Some people say that the greatest form of admiration is imitation. Choose to imitate God your Father as His beloved child. The Bible says, "Yet to all who did receive Him, to those who believed in His name, He gave the right to become children of God" (John 1:12 NIV). If you made the Great Exchange in faith, then you have received Him and believed in His name. You have the right to become a child of God, so be sure to imitate His heart and His actions. Get to know God, His character, and His ways by spending time in His Word and in His presence.

As you get to know God, learn the names He calls Himself in Scripture. God reveals His heart and character through His names: Healer, Provider, Love, Kindness, Merciful One, Father, Daddy, Gracious Redeemer, Savior, Deliverer, Restorer, Comforter, Creator, Refuge, Counselor, Prince of Peace, Mighty God, All Powerful, Sufficient One, Shield, Faithful, Beloved, Wonderful, Desire of the Nations, Beautiful One and many more. If you take time to speak to God using His names, and if you praise Him for being what those names mean in your life, you will grow in His love. Once you get a glimpse of His deep, abiding love for you, you will be transformed and changed forever.

God loves you with a perfect love. The Greek word for God's love for you is "agape." Your Heavenly Father's agape towards you is perfect, unconditional, and unselfish. If you have felt locked in a prison of distrust because people and life have let you down, then use the key of faith in God's agape love to unlock the door and walk out into glorious freedom.

MEDITATION/JOURNAL

Spend time meditating on the names of our King. Journal your thoughts.

_____

_____

_____

_____

_____

_____

_____

_____

_____

_____

_____

_____

_____

_____

THE CHALLENGE

Take time to speak to God using His names and praising him for who He shows Himself to be in every name.

_____

THE PRAYER

Father, help me to become like you. Help me to see who you are so that I may become like you as your dearly beloved child. Sometimes it is hard to see, feel and receive your love because of this unlovely world and its broken people. Help me to understand, receive, and then give your love to others. I want to be a loving person who displays Your love. Open the eyes of my heart to catch a glimpse of your Glory so I may be transformed and walk in Your love.

_____

THE TRANSFORMATION

How has God transformed an area of your life through today's lesson?

Week 6

I AM A SON OF A GOOD FATHER

IN CHRIST,

I AM BRILLIANT
I AM BOLD
I AM BRAVE
I AM BLESSED
I AM BELOVED

I AM
A SON OF A GOOD FATHER

AND AN
HEIR OF A GREAT KING

DAY 36

I AM A SON OF A GOOD FATHER

For it is by grace that you have been saved through faith; and that not of yourselves, it is the gift of God;
not as a result of works, so that no one may boast.
Ephesians 2:8-9 (NIV)

This is day 36 on our 50 day walk to transformation. You cannot be truly transformed until you have received salvation. Have you been saved? This is perhaps the most important question of your life because the answer affects not only this life but your life to come for all eternity.

In the verse above, it says "for it is by grace that you have been saved." What is grace? One definition is "unmerited favor"—like an undeserved or unearned gift. Grace is a free gift from God given through salvation as you put your faith in Christ. The good news is, you do not have to work for salvation. When we do not work for something, then we cannot brag about or take credit for it.

Salvation in Christ means you receive eternal life. You can have peace in Christ and with God the Father, who adopts you as His beloved son. When you receive the gift of salvation by faith, the King of Heaven becomes your Father and His Kingdom is your inheritance. It means when your body dies, you will be transformed, and transferred into the presence of the King in His Kingdom. It means that you are not an orphan but an heir to a divine inheritance beyond your wildest imagination.

If you have not accepted this priceless gift of salvation yet, accept it today. Salvation is the greatest gift you will ever receive; you will be forever grateful that you accepted it.

MEDITATION/JOURNAL

Think about God as a Good Father, and journal about how that makes you feel. Do you believe He is good, and that He wants to share His Kingdom with you?

_____

_____

_____

_____

_____

_____

_____

_____

_____

_____

_____

_____

_____

THE CHALLENGE

Memorize today's scripture. Speak this scripture over yourself.

THE PRAYER

Thank you, God, for making salvation a free gift I can choose to accept by faith.

THE TRANSFORMATION

How has God transformed an area of your life through today's lesson?

IN CHRIST,

I AM BRILLIANT
I AM BOLD
I AM BRAVE
I AM BLESSED
I AM BELOVED

I AM
A SON OF A GOOD FATHER

AND AN
HEIR OF A GREAT KING

DAY 37

I AM A SON OF A GOOD FATHER

If you declare with your mouth, "Jesus is Lord," and believe in your heart that God raised Him from the dead, you will be saved. For it is with your heart you believe and are justified, and it is with your mouth that you profess your faith and are saved.
Romans 10:9-10 (NIV)

Today's Bible verse gives specific instructions on how you can accept the free gift of salvation. First, declare (speak out or confess) with your mouth that Jesus is Lord. That means acknowledge His authority and rule not just over all of creation but over you as a new creation. When you receive salvation and are "born again," it means you become an entirely new creation living for His glory. It means that He is not only seated on the throne of Heaven, but He's also seated on the throne of your heart.

You must also believe in your heart that God raised Jesus from the dead. Something happens when you believe this and confess Jesus as Lord: you receive the salvation we discussed yesterday. Jesus, the one who was raised from the dead, actually becomes Lord of your heart and life. Jesus in you is the hope of glory and Heaven! This is what makes you "righteous," or right with God. The Bible says when we "receive the abundance of His Grace and the gift of righteousness," we shall be able to "reign in life through the one Christ Jesus" (Romans 5:17). Jesus has put everything under His feet, including death and the devil, and He is coming back soon to rule, reign, and make everything right. You can reign in this life now as you fully surrender to His reign in your heart.

Salvation is simple. Just say "Jesus is Lord," and believe in your heart that God raised Him from the dead, and you will be saved. After you have accepted Jesus as Lord of your life, the Bible instructs you to be baptized. Baptism is an act of faith and is an outward symbol of dying to your old life and being raised up into a new life in Christ. Jesus said, "Whosoever confesses Me before men, I will also confess him before My Father who is in Heaven. But whoever denies Me before men, I will also deny him before My Father who is in Heaven" (Matthew 10:32 NKJV). The act of baptism does not save you; it is an act of obedience, and it is a proclamation that you are choosing to follow Jesus. It symbolizes a new birth and a washing away of sins. After you have been saved and baptized, a whole new world of transformation is open to you!

MEDITATION/JOURNAL

Is it hard for you to publicly confess that Jesus is Lord? Why do you think that is? How can you overcome that? Journal your thoughts.

_____

_____

_____

_____

_____

_____

_____

_____

_____

_____

_____

_____

_____

THE CHALLENGE

If you believe in your heart that God has raised Jesus from the dead, confess him first as Lord to yourself and then to others. Be obedient in baptism as an act of faith and/or as an act of rededication to Christ.

THE PRAYER

Father, I choose to believe in my heart and publicly confess you with my mouth that you are Lord. I want to be baptized in Your name. Thank you for my salvation and transformation. Help me to follow You.

THE TRANSFORMATION

How has God transformed an area of your life through today's lesson?

IN CHRIST,

I AM BRILLIANT
I AM BOLD
I AM BRAVE
I AM BLESSED
I AM BELOVED

I AM
A SON OF A GOOD FATHER

AND AN
HEIR OF A GREAT KING

DAY 38

I AM A SON OF A GOOD FATHER

The Lord is the Spirit, and where the Spirit of the Lord is, there is freedom.
2 Corinthians 3:17 (NIV)

The Bible says "do not grieve the Spirit" but instead make the Spirit a welcome guest in your home (Ephesians 4:30). A prayer in the Bible for you is that God would "grant you, according to the riches of His glory, to be strengthened with power through His Spirit in the inner man, so that Christ may dwell in your hearts through faith" (Ephesians 3:16 NKJV). Another prayer is that you are "set free from bondage to corruption and obtain the glorious freedom" available to the children of God (Romans 8:21).

Not everyone who receives salvation accepts the freedom promised to them. Many Christians die and go to Heaven but spend their whole life in some sort of bondage. Salvation is free, but freedom comes at a cost. There is a cost to following Christ, and it includes dying to such things as falsehoods, unforgiveness, and selfishness. The good news is the cost is well worth it! Jesus said the cost of freedom and His Kingdom is like spending all you have for a field that contains one hidden pearl of great price and then going out and purchasing that field. It is as if you spent one hundred thousand dollars to receive one billion! The keys to freedom and the Kingdom of Heaven are hidden in Christ, who is in you. Christ in you is your hope for the glorious freedom He wants you to experience.

The Holy Spirit will dwell freely in you when you are aware of the Spirit and are careful to be in tune with the His leading. Jesus said, when we follow Him it is not burdensome because we live in the victory brought about by our faith in Him (1 John 5:3-4). Freedom is light and delightful. Captivity is hard and painful. Tune into the Spirit by singing praise songs to yourself throughout the day. The Bible says God is enthroned in His praises, and His angels are present wherever there is praise. You can also praise Him with spoken words, His Word and with your actions. When you choose the Lord, praise, and obedience, you choose light, joy, and freedom.

MEDITATION/JOURNAL

What are some areas in your life that are burdensome to you? Think about the truth that you can live a life of victory when you put your faith in Christ. How do your thoughts need to transform in order to see those burdens change to freedom? What action steps do you need to make? Journal your thoughts.

_____

_____

_____

_____

_____

_____

_____

_____

_____

_____

_____

_____

THE CHALLENGE

Praise God all through the day with your thoughts, words, songs, and actions. At the end of the day, see if you feel lighter and more free.

_____

THE PRAYER

Holy Spirit, I want to experience your glorious freedom. Help me to pay the cost to receive your riches. I invite you to dwell richly in and near me, for I believe there is freedom when you are present. Thank you for the present of your presence which brings freedom.

_____

THE TRANSFORMATION

How has God transformed an area of your life through today's lesson?

IN CHRIST,

I AM BRILLIANT
I AM BOLD
I AM BRAVE
I AM BLESSED
I AM BELOVED

I AM
A SON OF A GOOD FATHER

AND AN
HEIR OF A GREAT KING

DAY 39

I AM A SON OF A GOOD FATHER

Then you will know the truth, and the truth will set you free.
John 8:32 (NIV)

To know truth is to know true freedom. Jesus said, "I am the way, the truth, and the life. No one comes to the Father except through me" (John 14:6 NIV). He also said God's Word is truth. We also have access to the Holy Spirit which will guide us into all truth.

We attain true freedom when we get to know our Father as a beloved son. We do this by talking with Him daily, seeking His truth in His Word, and listening to the Holy Spirit's voice. The Hebrew word for "know" means getting to know the Lord so intimately that we become one with Him. This is somewhat similar to the sacred oneness that a loving husband and wife are meant to share. Jesus prayed that all Christians would be one with Him, just as He is one with the Father (John 17:20-21).

One of the first steps to freedom is to always tell the truth and stop lying. Being dishonest with others and yourself keeps you dissatisfied and in bondage. One practical way to find freedom in this area is to stop and apologize when you find yourself lying to someone. Correct yourself, and speak the truth instead. Once you have done this a few times, you will always want to tell the truth so you won't embarrass yourself! Keep in mind, being truthful does not mean speaking everything you think. You don't want to be hurtful to others, even when speaking the truth. Be wise with your words, and only speak truth in love. When you speak truth in love, you will feel lighter, cleaner, and so much better about yourself. You will be a true example of a faithful son of a Good Father.

MEDITATION/JOURNAL

Think about the times you have not been truthful, either by lying or by keeping back information. How did it make you feel? Journal your thoughts.

_____

_____

_____

_____

_____

_____

_____

_____

_____

_____

_____

_____

_____

THE CHALLENGE

Decide to seek truth and be truthful starting today. If you lie, correct yourself out loud.

THE PRAYER

Father, help me to know the truth and allow the truth to set me free.

THE TRANSFORMATION

How has God transformed an area of your life through today's lesson?

IN CHRIST,

I AM BRILLIANT
I AM BOLD
I AM BRAVE
I AM BLESSED
I AM BELOVED

I AM
A SON OF A GOOD FATHER

AND AN
HEIR OF A GREAT KING

DAY 40

I AM A SON OF A GOOD FATHER

But while he was still a long way off, his father saw him and was filled with compassion for him; he ran to his son, threw his arms around him and kissed him.
Luke 15:20 (NIV)

Today's scripture focuses on the prodigal son. He walked away from his father's house, demanding his inheritance. Then he wasted it on wicked and wild living. After nearly starving, he finally came to his senses and decided to return to his father's house. He knew he had dishonored, not only his father, but his family, by his actions.

Finally, he came to his senses and said, "I am no longer worthy to be called your son; make me like one of your hired servants." But while he was still a long way off, his father saw him and was filled with compassion for him; he ran to His son, threw his arms around him and kissed him. The father had his servants clothe him with the best robe, put a ring on his finger, and sandals on his feet. Then he had a feast to welcome him home. Instead of rejecting his son, the father celebrated his return (Luke 15:19-24, NIV).

Are you a long way away from your Father, or perhaps even feeling lost? Then return quickly to your Father and His house. He awaits your return and will run to meet you and restore your honored place. Humble yourself and admit you have sinned against your Father and heaven. Quickly repent and return to God. Our Abba Father wants us to be free from sin, not enslaved to it. Acts 2:38 tells us to "repent and be baptized, every one of you, in the name of Jesus Christ for the forgiveness of your sins" (NIV). Is God calling you to be baptized? After rededicating their lives to Him, some people choose to be re-baptized—even immersed in water as Jesus was.

MEDITATION/JOURNAL

Do you feel like you messed up so badly that the Father wouldn't take you back? Read today's scripture again, and let the truth of it become real to you. Your Father wants to run to you and welcome you back with open arms! Journal your thoughts.

THE CHALLENGE

If you are away from the Father and the family of God, return and come home. He is waiting to run, embrace, and restore you as His child. If you need to be baptized in water as an act of first-time obedience or rededication, do it!

THE PRAYER

Holy Spirit, I choose to repent and return wholeheartedly to right living. I want to dwell in the house of the Lord as His child and as part of the family of God.

THE TRANSFORMATION

How has God transformed an area of your life through today's lesson?

IN CHRIST,

I AM BRILLIANT
I AM BOLD
I AM BRAVE
I AM BLESSED
I AM BELOVED

I AM
A SON OF A GOOD FATHER

AND AN
HEIR OF A GREAT KING

DAY 41

I AM A SON OF A GOOD FATHER

For all have sinned and fall short of the glory of God.
Romans 3:23 (NIV)

Sometimes it's hard to imagine a "good father." Maybe you don't know your earthly father, or maybe your earthly father has hurt you. If so, you are not alone. In the Bible, God refers to King David as "a man after My own heart" (Acts:13:22 NIV), but David's earthly father would have scored pretty low on the Good Father scale!

In 1 Samuel 16, God tells the prophet Samuel that one of Jesse's sons will be the next king of Israel. Samuel asks Jesse to bring all of his sons before him. Jesse brought out seven of his sons, and Samuel considered each one, but he knew God hadn't chosen them. Samuel asked if Jesse had any more sons, and it turned out that he had never invited or even mentioned his youngest son, David. The very son that the father overlooked was actually the Lord's chosen! Samuel anointed David to become the next king of Israel, and he became one of the great heroes of the Bible: a famous warrior, king, and worshiper of his Father God. Jesus was even born into the lineage of David. That's a very impressive resume for an overlooked or forgotten son!

Regardless of your earthly father's thoughts and actions toward you, your Heavenly Father sees you, knows you, understands you, and has a good plan for your life. When we give our lives to Jesus, we are reconciled to our heavenly father, who is not like the image you may have of a dysfunctional, earthly father. He is even better than the world's best father. He is a perfect Father, in whom you can believe and trust, and He longs to accept you into His family.

MEDITATION/JOURNAL

Our Heavenly Father is our creator, so give Him thanks for the way He created you, including your health, intellect, talent, skills, etc. Thank Him for every gift, every blessing, every good thing in your life. Journal your thoughts.

_____

_____

_____

_____

_____

_____

_____

_____

_____

_____

_____

_____

_____

THE CHALLENGE

Between you and the Lord, admit that your earthly father is human and therefore imperfect.
Ask the Lord to forgive your father for all the ways he has failed you or hurt you.

THE PRAYER

Lord, thank you that you so loved the world that you gave your only begotten son Jesus, that
whosoever believes in Him will not perish, but have everlasting life. And thank You for being
my good Father.

THE TRANSFORMATION

How has God transformed an area of your life through today's lesson?

IN CHRIST,

I AM BRILLIANT
I AM BOLD
I AM BRAVE
I AM BLESSED
I AM BELOVED

I AM
A SON OF A GOOD FATHER

AND AN
HEIR OF A GREAT KING

DAY 42

I AM A SON OF A GOOD FATHER

*It is for freedom that Christ has set us free. Stand firm, then, and do not let
yourselves be burdened again by a yoke of slavery.*
Galatians 5:1 (NIV)

The very reason Christ died for you is so that you might live in His freedom. He does not want you burdened again by a yoke of slavery: slavery to sin, slavery to fear, slavery to self-hatred, slavery to doubt, slavery to performance and pleasing people, slavery to religion. Jesus said to "take His yoke upon you, for His yoke is easy and His burden is light" (Matthew 11:30).

God wants us free to do and be everything He created us to do and be. Ephesians 2:10 says, "we are God's masterpiece. He has created us anew in Christ Jesus, so we can do the good things he planned for us long ago" (NLT). His plan is for good things in our life; he doesn't want our lives to be a burden. Life can be hard, and you might not be happy every moment, but following Christ should still be a joy.

Isaiah 64:8 says: "Yet you, Lord, are our Father. We are the clay, you are the potter; we are all the work of your hand"(NIV). Just as a potter transforms clay, the Father desires to transform us into His Masterpiece. Our faithful Father promises that He will complete the good work in us (Philippians 1:6). However, if we remove ourselves from the potter's wheel, we may miss out on our Master's original design and end up as an incomplete work.

If we trust our Good Father, real transformations occur. Fear turns to faith, anxiety turns to peace, and stress turns to rest. Dishonor turns to honor, depression turns to joy, and disobedience turns to obedience. Rudeness turns to kindness. Dishonesty turns to honesty. Impatience turns to patience. Unfaithfulness turns to faithfulness. Out-of-control becomes self-control. Poverty turns to provision, foolishness turns to wisdom, and cowardice becomes courage. Timidity transforms into boldness, hatred becomes love, and hopelessness becomes hopefulness. Cursing turns to blessing, devastation becomes restoration, and victim becomes victor.

Your Heavenly Father wants to free you from everything that is not best for you. He wants to free you to receive, do, and become everything He created you for! Stand firm in your faith and in the freedom Christ has given you. You are worth it!!

MEDITATION/JOURNAL

Write down some recurring strongholds in your life, ones that seem to keep coming back up. Then ask the Lord to show you ways to conquer them with His freedom. Remember that you are God's masterpiece, created for good things, and that He doesn't want you to put the yoke of slavery to sin back on! Journal your thoughts.

_____

_____

_____

_____

_____

_____

_____

_____

_____

_____

_____

_____

_____

THE CHALLENGE

Decide once and for all to walk fully in the freedom Christ purchased for you on the Cross. Stand firm against any slavery that you face.

THE PRAYER

Father, help me to answer your call to experience your freedom in every area of my life, now and for the rest of my life. Help me to be fully transformed.

THE TRANSFORMATION

How has God transformed an area of your life through today's lesson?

Week 7

I AM AN HEIR OF A GREAT KING

IN CHRIST,

I AM BRILLIANT
I AM BOLD
I AM BRAVE
I AM BLESSED
I AM BELOVED

I AM
A SON OF A GOOD FATHER

AND AN
AN HEIR OF A GREAT KING

DAY 43

I AM AN HEIR OF A GREAT KING

The Spirit himself testifies with our spirit that we are God's children. Now if we are children, then we are heirs—heirs of God and co-heirs with Christ, if indeed we share in his sufferings in order that we may also share in his glory.
Romans 8:16-17 (NIV)

This is day 43 on our 50 day walk to transformation. Transformation occurs through salvation and a deeply-rooted understanding of your identity as a child of a Good Father. You should then be baptized into His Son Jesus Christ, taking your place as an heir in His Kingdom.

An heir is someone who has the right to receive an inheritance (land, rights, wealth, or possessions) from the previous owner—usually their parent—as a gift. The scripture above reminds us that if we are the Father's children, we are also His heirs. In fact, we are called co-heirs with Christ. God is the Creator, and He has the right to treat us as mere creatures. Instead, He welcomes us as fully-adopted children with inheritance rights to His kingdom.

In scripture, Paul seems to include a condition of inheritance: "suffering with Christ." However, some translate this not as a condition but a presupposition—since we are heirs with Christ, we will suffer with Him. Jesus himself said, "...In this world you will have tribulation, but be of good cheer, I have overcome the world" (John 16:33, NKJV).

So what does it mean to "share in His sufferings"? It means to be persecuted because of our close identity with Christ (John 15:20); dying to ourselves (Romans 6:5-8); and glorifying God in the midst of living in a sin-scarred world. The wonderful news is we will be rewarded in our suffering. In fact, the Bible entreats us to rejoice in our sufferings, knowing that they produce endurance, character, and hope (Romans 5:3-4). Suffering also produces perseverance, maturity, and completeness (James 1:2-4). Our Bridegroom King promised the gift of the crown of life to those who are faithful to suffer even to the point of death (Revelation 2:10). We will explore the other priceless gifts included in our rich inheritance as His Eternal Heirs during the rest of this week.

MEDITATION/JOURNAL

What does it mean to you to know that you are an heir in God's Kingdom, and a joint-heir with Christ? Journal your thoughts.

_____

_____

_____

_____

_____

_____

_____

_____

_____

_____

_____

_____

_____

_____

_____

THE CHALLENGE

Memorize today's scripture. Speak this scripture over yourself.

THE PRAYER

Thank you, God, for being a Good Father and a Great King. Help me to repent wholeheartedly and cause the transformational truth of who I am in You to root deeply in my heart and life.

THE TRANSFORMATION

How has God transformed an area of your life through today's lesson?

IN CHRIST,

I AM BRILLIANT
I AM BOLD
I AM BRAVE
I AM BLESSED
I AM BELOVED

I AM
A SON OF A GOOD FATHER

AND AN
AN HEIR OF A GREAT KING

DAY 44

I AM AN HEIR OF A GREAT KING

I am going to send you what my Father has promised; but stay in the city
until you have been clothed with power from on high.
Luke 24:49 (NIV)

As an Heir of a Great King, the Lord desires you to be royally robed in His power! He desires you to receive the gift of the Holy Spirit in all His fullness, so that you are clothed with the same power that raised Jesus from the dead (Romans 6:4). Then, through His power, you will heal the sick and the broken-hearted, make disciples, and even perform miracles.

As His Heir, you have received a mighty gift of power, and it is your responsibility to handle your inheritance with care. Every gift He has given you is for His kingdom and His glory! To use those gifts for your own benefit, to hide or neglect them, would not honor the One who gave them to you. Instead, maximize the Father's gifts so He will say to you, "Well done, good and faithful servant; you have been faithful over a few things, I will make you ruler over many things. Enter into the joy of your lord" (Matthew 25:23, NKJV).

When you believe and are baptized, you are sealed with the Holy Spirit and the promise of salvation as a son of the King (Ephesians 1:13). But you can also receive the power of the Holy Spirit in fuller measure. Consider this verse in Matthew 3:11 (NIV) where John the Baptist says, "I baptize you with water for repentance. But after me comes one who is more powerful than I...He will baptize you with the Holy Spirit and fire." In Acts 2:3-4, we learn that the fire and power of the Holy Spirit came at Pentecost. He offers the gift of the Spirit without measure (John 3:34) to those who obey (Acts 5:32). As the King's Heir, ask for the power of the Holy Spirit, obey God's directions, and wait expectantly for a greater manifestation of the outpouring of His Spirit's power upon you.

MEDITATION/JOURNAL

Imagine the Father placing a heavenly royal robe of power on you to show you how you are to present yourself as an Heir of a Great King. Journal your thoughts.

_____

_____

_____

_____

_____

_____

_____

_____

_____

_____

_____

_____

_____

_____

THE CHALLENGE

Ask for a greater manifestation of the Holy Spirit in power. Then wait. If you do not receive it today, ask again and every day until you do!

THE PRAYER

Father, help me to see myself as an Heir of a Great King! Lead me daily and show me how to walk as if I am robed in Your power.

THE TRANSFORMATION

How has God transformed an area of your life through today's lesson?

IN CHRIST,

I AM BRILLIANT
I AM BOLD
I AM BRAVE
I AM BLESSED
I AM BELOVED

I AM
A SON OF A GOOD FATHER

AND AN
AN HEIR OF A GREAT KING

DAY 45

I AM AN HEIR OF A GREAT KING

I pray that...you may know...the riches of his glorious inheritance in his holy people,
and his incomparably great power for us who believe. That power is the same as the mighty strength he
exerted when he raised Christ from the dead . . .
Ephesians 1:18-20 (NIV)

This scripture from Ephesians 1 is God's prayer written by Paul for you, His Heir. The inheritance available to you is a delightful inheritance (Psalm16:6), beyond what you could ask or imagine, according to Ephesians 3:20. It is a vast, incorruptible inheritance (1 Peter 1:4) which includes every spiritual blessing in Christ (Ephesians 1:13), as well as the Holy Spirit, who is sent to empower, guide, counsel, and comfort you. You also inherit angelic assistance (Psalm 91:11), answered prayers of faith in accordance with His will (1 John 5:14), the kingdom of heaven (Matthew 25:34), the nations (Psalm 2:8), and the gifts of the Spirit (1 Corinthians 12). We are even promised a home in heaven prepared for us by Christ (John 14:3). This should ignite a passion in us to possess our promised inheritance!

The key to unlocking your kingdom inheritance is faith. The Bible says that faith is a gift (Ephesians 2:8-10), yet it also says our work is produced by faith (1 Thessalonians 1:3). Faith can be both a gift and a work. Consider someone who has a musical gift, such as Mozart. If he had not worked at that gift, his potential may never have been fully realized.

Have faith that actually works by working out your faith (James 2:22). It is your King's desire that by faith you would unlock your full inheritance and the gifts available to you. May you choose to fully access your inheritance and power so that you represent your Father, the King, as His true "HRH" - His Royal Heir!

MEDITATION/JOURNAL

Ask the Lord to show you your inheritance and what it looks like to walk in faith. Journal your thoughts.

_____

_____

_____

_____

_____

_____

_____

_____

_____

_____

_____

_____

_____

_____

_____

THE CHALLENGE

God's Word is the official legal document of your inheritance. Study it daily.

THE PRAYER

Father, empower me to be a good steward of my full inheritance. Help me to have the kind of faith that ushers in this glorious inheritance!

THE TRANSFORMATION

How has God transformed an area of your life through today's lesson?

IN CHRIST,

I AM BRILLIANT
I AM BOLD
I AM BRAVE
I AM BLESSED
I AM BELOVED

I AM
A SON OF A GOOD FATHER

AND AN
AN HEIR OF A GREAT KING

DAY 46

I AM AN HEIR OF A GREAT KING

For the sin of this one man, Adam, caused death to rule over many. But even greater is God's wonderful grace and his gift of righteousness, for all who receive it will live in triumph over sin and death through this one man, Jesus Christ.
Romans 5:17 (NLT)

Our Savior's finished work on the cross not only conquered death, but also purchased our ransom from slavery. He also qualified us—the unqualified—to be kings for the glory and the kingdom of our Father, the King of kings (Revelation 1:6). What a great exchange! Death for life. Slavery for reigning.

Jesus said, "Anyone who loves their life will lose it, while anyone who hates their life in this world will keep it for eternal life" (John 12:25, NIV). Our Savior also said, "The greatest among you will be your servant. For those who exalt themselves will be humbled, and those who humble themselves will be exalted" (Matthew 23:11, NIV).

When we receive His grace—unmerited favor—we receive supernatural favor, ability, and anointing that we have not earned or deserved. When we receive the righteousness of Christ—His perfection and holiness—this qualifies us, the unqualified, to reign in life. Our life in Christ is a paradox: while serving, we rule; we labor, yet we rest; we are to be strong, yet weak; rich, yet poor.

What does it look like to reign in life? First, we must receive and rest in the free gift of His righteousness and grace. When we remain in Him, we will not only bear much fruit, but it is fruit that will never spoil or ruin (John 15), specifically, the fruit of the Spirit: love, joy, peace, patience, kindness, goodness, gentleness, faithfulness, and self-control in our heart, home, and life (Galatians 5:22-23). We do all of this with the humility of a child (Matthew 18:4) and a servant, like our Savior, Jesus Christ (Philippians 2:7).

MEDITATION/JOURNAL

Imagine yourself reigning in life. Journal your thoughts.

_____

_____

_____

_____

_____

_____

_____

_____

_____

_____

_____

_____

_____

_____

_____

_____

THE CHALLENGE

Study the scriptures above on rest and reigning.

THE PRAYER

Father, help me to receive your abundant grace and the gift of your righteousness so I might reign in life through Christ Jesus.

THE TRANSFORMATION

How has God transformed an area of your life through today's lesson?

IN CHRIST,

I AM BRILLIANT
I AM BOLD
I AM BRAVE
I AM BLESSED
I AM BELOVED

I AM
A SON OF A GOOD FATHER

AND AN
AN HEIR OF A GREAT KING

DAY 47

I AM AN HEIR OF A GREAT KING

But you are a chosen people, a royal priesthood, a holy nation, God's special possession, that you may declare the praises of him who called you out of darkness into his wonderful light.
1 Peter 2:9 (NIV)

Part of our inheritance includes walking in freedom. We must come out from the bondage of darkness into His glorious light. The book of Hosea tells us that for lack of knowledge, His people perish (Hosea 4:6). Knowing and applying His truth is the key to truly setting us free from the bondage of depression, addiction, striving, falsehood, people-pleasing, lust, lack, generational curses, greed, and any other strongholds that have taken hold in our lives. As we come out of bondage and into the light, we have fellowship with one another and are covered by the blood of Jesus.

In fellowship, we should confess our sins to one another and pray for one another that we may be healed (James 5:16). An important key to walking in the light is regularly meeting with our family in Christ—other royal sons and daughters of our King and Father (Hebrews 10:25). It is important to regularly take communion—union with the body of Christ—as a part of our worship (Acts 2:42), as well as commune with (spend time with) our Christian family.

This week we have learned about the magnitude of our inheritance. In the last book of the Bible, it is revealed that the one who overcomes will inherit "all things" (Revelation 21:7). Ultimately, our highest inheritance is Him—Jesus our Bridegroom King—and eternity spent with Him.

Do you realize that you are also a treasured inheritance to your King? He has called you to reign brilliantly, boldly, and bravely as the beloved and blessed son of a Good Father and Heir of a Great King, all to His glory. You will be a crown in the hand of the Lord (Isaiah 62:3). Seek your full inheritance with all your heart; but most of all, seek your ultimate treasure—your Bridegroom King, your Good Father, and the Holy Spirit.

MEDITATION/JOURNAL

Meditate on today's scripture and what it means to be God's treasured inheritance.

_____

_____

_____

_____

_____

_____

_____

_____

_____

_____

_____

_____

_____

_____

_____

_____

_____

THE CHALLENGE

Beyond this study, seek the King, His Spirit, and your inheritance with your whole heart. Be willing to come out of the darkness into His light. When you do, He promises to help you find what you are looking for.

THE PRAYER

Lord, help me to be your treasured inheritance, to come out of darkness, and to walk in the light. Help me talk about your excellence everywhere I go.

THE TRANSFORMATION

How has God transformed an area of your life through today's lesson?

IN CHRIST,

I AM BRILLIANT
I AM BOLD
I AM BRAVE
I AM BLESSED
I AM BELOVED

I AM
A SON OF A GOOD FATHER

AND AN
AN HEIR OF A GREAT KING

DAY 48

I AM AN HEIR OF A GREAT KING

You, my brothers and sisters, were called to be free. But do not use your freedom to indulge the flesh; rather, serve one another humbly in love.
Galatians 5:13 (NIV)

You were given salvation, and you are called to freedom. God still loves you when you mess up, make mistakes and even outright sin. You don't lose your salvation when you sin. In fact, the Bible says when we fall into sin, we are called to get right back up. When you sin, confess your sin, and God will be faithful to forgive you. However, if we continue to live a life of selfish sin without a heart for transformation, we will live in bondage instead of the freedom of salvation.

You are not called to captivity; you are called to be free and to live free. The only thing that needs to be in captivity is any thought or action that is not obedient to Christ. As we discussed last week, when you complete the Great Exchange and daily exchange your life for His, you will walk into the riches of His glorious freedom.

Once you surrender your life completely to Him, choose to humbly serve others with a heart of love. Serving yourself puts you in bondage. You experience freedom when you serve Christ and others. Jesus said if you want to be great, you must be the servant of all (Mark 9:35). Serve with the heart of a King and rule with the heart of a servant. Whenever you serve others, you are serving Christ. That is why the Bible says whatever you do, do it with excellence and wholeheartedly because you are really serving God and not humans (Colossians 3:23). You will find freedom as you serve Christ and allow Him to be the master and ruler of your heart and life.

MEDITATION/JOURNAL

What are some ways you serve only yourself? What are some ways you can serve other people, and the Lord? Journal your thoughts.

_____

_____

_____

_____

_____

_____

_____

_____

_____

_____

_____

_____

_____

_____

THE CHALLENGE

Choose to answer the call to freedom today by serving others humbly in love.

THE PRAYER

My Father and King, live and reign through me. I want to be more than a conqueror over sin and selfishness. Help me make the Great Exchange and never turn back. I want to belong to you and you to me. Let me never be separated from your love.

THE TRANSFORMATION

How has God transformed an area of your life through today's lesson?

IN CHRIST,

I AM BRILLIANT
I AM BOLD
I AM BRAVE
I AM BLESSED
I AM BELOVED

I AM
A SON OF A GOOD FATHER

AND AN
AN HEIR OF A GREAT KING

DAY 49

I AM AN HEIR OF A GREAT KING

Let us therefore come boldly to the throne of grace, that we may obtain
mercy and find grace to help in time of need.
Hebrews 4:16 (NKJV)

The word of God says we can come boldly before the throne as joint heirs (Romans 8:17). If you have a need, ask the Lord to help you. Sometimes the most powerful prayer we can pray is simply, "Lord, help me!"

Sometimes we will suffer in this life, but it does not mean that the Lord has forgotten about us or left us. It may be that we are going through a time of testing, and we need to learn something from the situation, such as how to turn to God, or how to rely on Him more and to draw closer to Him. It's in those moments that we need to stay in the Word daily and in prayer.

Your Heavenly Father wants you to come to Him with everything you're going through, whether it's small or great. He wants you to have bold access to His throne, as a beloved son. And once you've come into His Presence, He will extend grace to help you in your time of need.

Remember that you are an Heir! Your handbook for how to receive your inheritance and how to walk out the role of an Heir is the Bible! Hebrews 4:12 says, "For the word of God is living and powerful, and sharper than any two-edged sword, piercing even to the division of soul and spirit, and of joints and marrow, and is a discerner of the thoughts and intents of the heart" (NKJV). If you are continually in the Word, you will know Him more intimately and He will continue to do a good work in you. Read the word when you are in times of trouble, when you need to hear from God, and on a daily basis. Spend time asking the Lord to reveal in you the things that He would like to help you change.

The word of God will help you discern your thoughts and the intentions of your heart.

MEDITATION/JOURNAL

Imagine yourself boldly coming before God's throne with your prayers and needs. See Him extend His grace to you as a beloved son and heir. Journal your thoughts.

_____

_____

_____

_____

_____

_____

_____

_____

_____

_____

_____

_____

_____

THE CHALLENGE

Relationships take time, so make sure to make the time for your relationship with the Father each day. Keep in the Word daily and pray daily.

THE PRAYER

Lord, help me to come to you in my time of need, but also each day. When I forget to spend time with you, please gently remind me by your Holy Spirit to come to you. I pray that you would help me to grow and to continually change and become more like you.

THE TRANSFORMATION

How has God transformed an area of your life through today's lesson?

IN CHRIST,

I AM BRILLIANT
I AM BOLD
I AM BRAVE
I AM BLESSED
I AM BELOVED

I AM
A SON OF A GOOD FATHER

AND AN
AN HEIR OF A GREAT KING

DAY 50

I AM AN HEIR OF A GREAT KING

And we all, who with unveiled faces contemplate the Lord's glory, are being transformed into His image with ever increasing glory, which comes from the Lord, who is the Spirit.
2 Corinthians 3:18 (NIV)

Congratulations! You persevered through *50 Days to Transformation*! The goal is not perfection, but progress, as you continue to be transformed into His image with ever-increasing glory.

In the Bible, fifty is the number for Jubilee, which is a time of being freed from slavery, debt, and disappointment. It is also a time of release, restoration of liberty, rest, and fruitful blessing in your inherited promised land. This is the hope for you and your future generations as Galatians 6:9 says: you will reap a harvest if you do not give up.

Take time to savor and celebrate your victory by remembering how far you have come. With a renewed mind, visualize yourself living out your glorious transformation. May you experience true Jubilee rest, freedom from all bondage, and complete restoration of your full inheritance, because Jesus came to be your Jubilee!

In fact, every year can be a year of the Lord's favored time of Jubilee for you, the transformed believer in Yeshua (Luke 4; Isaiah 61; 2 Corinthians 1:20). Well done! Your Father is well pleased. You have renewed your mind over these fifty days by immersing yourself in the consistent meditation on His word and in prayer.

Congratulations and blessings on your ever-unfolding transformation in Christ! You are hereby commissioned as a Brilliant, Bold, Brave, Blessed, Beloved Son of a Good Father, and Heir of a Great King! Rise and shine as you take up your royal position, daily walking and growing in your transformation, for the King and His glory!

MEDITATION/JOURNAL

Congratulations on completing this 50 day program! Reflect on your transformation journey. Journal your breakthroughs and your progress towards knowing who God is and how wonderful you are in Christ.

_____

_____

_____

_____

_____

_____

_____

_____

_____

_____

_____

_____

_____

_____

THE CHALLENGE

Reflect on your journey over the last seven weeks.
Have these topics transformed your thinking and decisions?

- Brilliant – daily renew your mind in the Word, and worship during your daily Power Hour.

- Bold – stand up for what is right, even when it's difficult or unpopular.

- Brave – courageously overcome and be more than a conqueror, despite how you feel.

- Beloved – you are dearly loved by God and are part of His family.

- Blessed – receive a greater manifestation of His Spirit and power so you will be "blessed to be a blessing" as His witness to the ends of the Earth.

- Son of a Good Father – walk daily in your identity in Christ and in unity with your family.

- Heir of a Great King – reign in life by receiving the fullness of your gifts and inheritance when you daily surrender to the kingship of your Lord Jesus.

THE PRAYER

Lord, I'm in awe of how great You are! Thank you for sending Your only son Jesus to pay the price for my sins. Thank You that in Christ I am Brilliant, Bold, Brave, Blessed, Beloved, a Son of a Good Father, and an Heir of a Great King!

THE TRANSFORMATION

Now that you have completed your 50 Days to Tranformation, who will you encourage to do the same?

ABOUT THE AUTHORS

Barbara Ann Jeter is Co-Founder as well as Co-President of Eternal Heir/ Heiress Ministries. She is an award-winning, top producing Realtor with experience as an educator and in marriage and family therapy. She strives to see every person find their true worth in Christ. She lives in Nashville, TN, with her beloved husband Charles, and is the adoring mother of her son Justin, daughter-in-love Grace, and daughter Georganna.

Mandy Arledge is Co-Founder and Co-President of Eternal Heir/Heiress Ministries. She is a Registered Nurse and a successful business owner, wife, and mother of two girls. Eternal Heir/Heiress Ministries is a vision she had to bring hope and encouragement to troubled and broken youth. With a difficult upbringing, her heart is to teach others how to find and follow God's purpose and plan even through trials and tribulations.

Nise Davies serves on the board of directors for Eternal Heir/Heiress Ministries. She is a producer and casting director for faith-based, family-friendly films, as well as an Arbonne Executive National Vice President. After a successful personal career as a model and actress, she established Advantage Models & Talent, the first openly Christian talent agency. Her mission is to change culture through faith-based films and media, and to help people become the best version of themselves.

Eternal Heir/Heiress Ministries was founded as a way to raise funds for the care of orphans, to raise awareness for and fund the plight of impoverished women and children, and to build the self esteem and character of young men and women by teaching them their value as an Eternal Heir or Heiress of their Heavenly Father, the King of Kings.

ACKNOWLEDGMENTS

Barbara Ann, Mandy, and Nise, as well as Eternal Heir/Heiress Ministries, would like to express their appreciation to all those who have truly made a difference in seeing the King of King's mission accomplished through this discipleship study material and in the ministry. We were only able to mention a few, but there are so many more unnamed individuals! Thank you to:

Our husbands: Charles Jeter, Marshall Arledge, and Brad Davies.

Ashley Hagan, Bayley Holt, and Brian Kannard, for all of the editing, design, and publishing details.

Becki Fortner and Prayer Avenue, including Susan West, for all your prayer power that truly helped make this not only fruitful, but possible.

All of our Power Hour Partners and Eternal Heirs and Heiresses.

Our Board members: Jola Moore and Laura Connor.

Our Advisory Board members: Blu Wyatt, April Burton, Edye Bisagno, Missy Maxwell, Cheryl Brown, Lenore Gilbert, Shaloma Wease, Phebe Esparza Frizbee, Selene Daniels, Rhonda Madge, Kate Battistelli, Margaret "Pearl" Roberts, Beckah Shea, Jen Wallace, Paula Wallace, Lisa Dinks, Dabney Mann, Becki Fortner, Jessica Scholes, Latoya Lackey, Julie True, Julie Smith, Patricia Douglas, India Goostree, Lynn Eldridge, and Glenda Sutton.

All our 50 Days Teachers and Volunteer Teams through the years, especially Wes and Beatriz Boggs, Eman Norman, Jason Kenyon, Dr. Jeffrey Moore, David Dantzler, Robert Kirkwood, Quinten Wilson, Tim and Crystal Romero, Mary Pryor, Blu Wyatt, Patricia and Mark Douglas, Selene Daniels, Lyndi and Russell Wills, Tim and Edye Bisagno, Billy Gaines, Candace Nosetine, Gigi and Rayne Arledge, Chris and Jen Wallace, Paula Wallace, and Julie Smith.

Lynn Eldridge, our Heir Force Prayer Team Leader; Bob Perry, Amy Lykosh and Workplace Prayer, our Prophetic Intercessors: Debra Jean, Celia Joy, and Peggy Adams, and our Gospel Partners, including Mandy Blum and Bonnie Gloth.

Special thanks to the churches and pastors who have partnered with us and encouraged us over the years: Harvest Sound, Pastors Sarah and Scott Macleod; New Song Nashville, Pastors Dale and Joan Evrist, and John Hall; Grace Chapel, Pastor Steve and Sarah Berger; Bethel World Outreach, Pastor Michael Williams and Pastor Dr. James Lowe; The Gate, Pastors Steve and Nancy Fry, and Adam Narcisco; Apostle Lenora Gilbert; Tim Bisagno; MXTV, Pastor Jaya and the young heirs in Tanku, India.

All the staff and workers in Nashville Detention Centers, and the detention center youth who went through 50 Days, made decisions for Christ, and those who were baptized.